Home & Family
Solicitor

First edition 1998
Reprinted 1998

Law Pack Publishing Limited
10-16 Cole Street
London SE1 4YH

Copyright © 1998 Law Pack Publishing

ISBN 1 898217 971

IMPORTANT FACTS ABOUT THIS LAW PACK BOOK

Law Pack publications are designed to provide authoritative and accurate information on the subject matter covered. However, neither this nor any other publication can take the place of a solicitor on important legal matters.

This **Law Pack** publication is sold on the understanding that the publisher, author and retailer are not engaged in rendering legal services. If legal advice or other expert assistance is required, the services of a competent professional should be sought.

The forms included in this **Law Pack** publication cover many everyday matters, but we cannot cater for all circumstances. If what you want is not included, we advise you to see a solicitor.

This **Law Pack** publication is designed only for use in England and Wales. It is not suitable for Scotland or Northern Ireland.

The information this book contains has been carefully compiled from reliable sources but its accuracy is not guaranteed as laws and regulations may change or be subject to differing interpretations. The law is stated as at 1 January 1998.

As with any legal matter, common sense should determine whether you need the assistance of a solicitor rather than relying solely on the information and forms in this **Law Pack** book.

We strongly urge you to consult a solicitor whenever substantial amounts of money are involved, or where you do not understand the instructions or are uncertain how to complete and use a form correctly, or if you have any doubts about its adequacy to protect you, or if what you want to do is not precisely covered by the forms provided.

© 1998 **Law Pack Publishing Limited**

PRINTED IN GREAT BRITAIN
LAW PACK PUBLISHING LIMITED
10-16 COLE STREET LONDON SE1 4YH

About Home & Family Solicitor...

This book contains ready-to-use legal letters and agreements to safeguard your legal rights and protect you, your family and your property.

With many essential legal documents in one book, you now have available the protection you need in simple legal matters without the inconvenience or cost of using a solicitor.

Law Pack publications are the ideal way to 'get it in writing'. What better way is there to document your important transactions, avoid costly disputes and enforce your legal rights? In a few minutes you can draw up the legal form or agreement you need to sidestep misunderstandings, comply with legal obligations and avoid liability.

How to use Home & Family Solicitor

It is easy to use **Law Pack's** *Home & Family Solicitor* by following these simple instructions:

1 To find the appropriate letter or agreement read the two tables of contents. The first lists each form alphabetically. The second groups them by subject.

2 You may find several documents for the same general purpose. To choose the form most appropriate for your specific needs, consult the Glossary, beginning on Page 203, as a guide to the purpose of each form. It is beyond the scope of *Home & Family Solicitor* to provide detailed information on the different areas of the law covered. But the content of each letter or agreement will alert you to the relevant legislation and indicate what your rights and remedies are.

3 Cut out and photocopy the document you want and keep the original so it can be used again in the future. Alternatively you can use the document as a template to prepare your own. Letter-type documents can be personalised by being reproduced on your own home letterhead.

4 Complete each document fully. Make certain all blanks (name, address, dates, amounts) are filled in. You may need to delete or add provisions in some documents to suit your requirements, especially where you find different options in [ ] brackets. If this is necessary, make sure each deletion or insertion is initialled by all parties. If there is not enough space on the document to make your insertion, it is best to type out the entire document, including the insertion, on a new sheet of paper.

5 Some documents have footnoted instructions, which should be observed if your are to use the document properly. Some documents refer to others in *Home & Family Solicitor,* or to other documents or copies of documents which will need to be attached before use.

About Deeds and Agreements

Under English law a contract does not have to be written down to be valid and enforceable. A verbal contract has just as much validity as a written contract. The problem associated with a verbal contract is that if there is a dispute over the contract the only evidence of the terms of the contract is the verbal evidence of each party to the contract which will be based on memory.

The reason that important contracts are written down, therefore, is so that a written record exists of what was agreed between the parties, to minimise the possibility of later disputes.

A contract exists where two or more parties make mutual promises to each other to take some sort of action or to make some payment to each other. An exchange of goods for money is the simplest form of contract. A simple promise by A to B, however, is not a contract, because B has given no "consideration" to A's promise. In order to turn A's promise into an enforceable contract B must also make some promise or payment in return (the consideration). A contract like this involving mutual promises can be referred to as both a contract and an agreement, and both terms are used to mean the same thing in *Home & Family Solicitor.*

It is sometimes the case that a simple promise by one party to another is all that two parties wish to record. The acceptance of such a promise is an agreement, but it is not enforceable because the other party has given no consideration for the promise. Such an agreement can be made enforceable if it is recorded in what is referred to as a deed. A deed is a written agreement which is given legal enforceability by the use of the word "deed".

An agreement recorded in a deed is enforceable in law regardless of whether mutual promises are made or not. You will find many of the agreements in *Home & Family Solicitor* are set up as deeds to make them enforceable.

Signature of Agreements. The part of an agreement or deed that the parties sign is known as the attestation clause. *In simple agreements, the attestation clause is the same for both parties.* Each party should sign the agreement and also get a witness to sign and provide his or her name and address.

Signature of Deeds. *In deeds, the attestation clauses are different for companies and individuals.* On each deed there is space for two individuals to sign, or two companies, or a combination of the two, depending on who is drawing up the deed. Each party should sign the deed and get a witness to sign and provide his or her name and address.

Use caution and common sense when using *Home & Family Solicitor*—or any other do-it-yourself legal product. Whilst these forms are generally considered appropriate for self-use, you must nevertheless decide when you should seek professional legal advice instead. You should consult a solicitor if:

- You need a complex or important agreement.
- Your transaction involves substantial amounts of money or expensive property.
- You don't understand how to use a document—or question its adequacy to protect you fully.

Because we cannot be certain that the forms in this book are appropriate to your circumstances —or are being properly used—we cannot assume any liability or responsibility in connection with their use.

TABLE OF CONTENTS

A

B

C

D

E

F

G

H

I

L

M

N

O

P

TABLE OF CONTENTS
by Category

I. Credit & Finance

II. Employment

III. Goods & Services

IV. Insurance

V. Personal

VI. Lettings & Property

VII. Local Environment

VIII. Miscellaneous

ACCIDENT CLAIM

Date _____

To _____

_____

_____

Ref _____

Dear _____

You are hereby notified of a claim against you for damages arising from the following accident or injury, to which I believe you and/or your agents are liable.

Description of Accident:

_____

_____

_____

Date _____

Time _____

Location _____

Please ask your insurance company or solicitor to contact me as soon as possible.

Yours sincerely

_____

Name _____

Address _____

_____

Tel. _____

1

ACCIDENT CLAIM: OCCUPIER'S LIABILITY

Date _____

To _____

_____

_____

Ref _____

Dear _____

On the above date, I was involved in an accident at your_____

_____, located at _____.

The following took place: _____

_____

_____

This was a result of:_____

_____

_____

This accident was a direct result of your negligence and failure to maintain a reasonable degree of safety on your premises. As it is quite clear that you failed to take reasonable safety precautions, as required by the Occupiers' Liability Act 1957, I am holding you liable for this accident.

I am entitled by law to receive compensation from you for the pain and suffering I endured as a consequence of this accident. I will expect to receive your proposals for the settlement of this claim within the next 10 days and trust we shall resolve this matter swiftly.

Yours sincerely

Name _____

Address _____

_____

Tel. _____

ADDRESS CHANGE NOTICE

Date _____

To _____

_____

_____

Dear _____

Ref _____

Please note that as from _____ 19 _____, our address will

change from:

_____

_____

_____

to

_____

_____

_____

Our new telephone number will be: _____ and fax: _____

Please make note of the above information and direct all future correspondence to us at our

new address. Thank you.

Yours sincerely

_____

AFFIDAVIT

I, _____ (name)

of _____ (address)

_____ (occupation)

MAKE OATH and say as follows:

_____

_____

_____

_____

_____

_____

_____

_____

_____

_____

_____

_____

_____
Signature

SWORN AT _____

        (address)

this _____ day of _____ 19 _____

before me,

_____
(A Solicitor or Commissioner for Oaths)

AFFIDAVIT OF POWER OF ATTORNEY

I,_____ of _____, make oath and

say as follows:

1.   The Power of Attorney granted to me by _____,

       on _____, a true copy of which is annexed hereto, is in full

       force and effect.

2.   That at the time of the execution of _____,

       on _____ I had no knowledge of or actual notice of the revoca-

       tion or termination of the Power of Attorney by death or otherwise.

3.   I make this affidavit for the purpose of inducing _____

       to accept the above described instrument as executed by me as attorney knowing that

       in accepting the aforesaid instrument they will rely upon this affidavit.

_____

Signature

SWORN AT _____

                (address)

this _____ day of _____ 19 _____

before me,

_____

(A Solicitor or Commissioner for Oaths)

AFFIDAVIT OF TITLE

I, _____(name)

of _____ (address)

_____(occupation)

MAKE OATH and say as follows:

1. I certify that I am now in possession of and am the absolute owner of the following property_____

_____

2. I also state that its possession has been undisputed and that I know of no fact or reason that may prevent transfer of this property to the buyer.

3. I also state that no liens, contracts, debts, or lawsuits exist regarding this property, except the following_____

4. I finally state that I have full power to transfer full title to this property to the buyer.

_____

Signature

SWORN AT _____

(address)

this _____day of _____ 19 _____

before me,

_____

(A Solicitor or Commissioner for Oaths)

AGREEMENT

THIS AGREEMENT is made the _____ day of _____ 19_____

BETWEEN:

(1) _____ of _____ (the "First Party"); and

(2) _____ of _____ (the "Second Party").

NOW IT IS HEREBY AGREED as follows:

1. That in consideration of the mutual covenants and agreements to be kept and performed on the part of said parties hereto, respectively as herein stated, the First Party hereby covenants and agrees that it shall:

_____

_____

_____

_____

_____

_____

2. And the Second Party hereby covenants and agrees that it shall:

_____

_____

_____

_____

_____

_____

3. Other terms to observed by and between the parties:

_____

_____

_____

_____

_____

4. This agreement shall be binding upon the parties, their successors and assigns. This is the entire agreement.

IN WITNESS OF WHICH the parties have signed this agreement the day and year first above written.

_____

Signed by or on behalf of the First Party

_____

in the presence of (witness)

Name _____

Address _____

_____

Occupation _____

_____

Signed by or on behalf of the Second Party

_____

in the presence of (witness)

Name _____

Address _____

_____

Occupation _____

ANTI-GAZUMPING AGREEMENT

(an Exclusivity Contract between the Buyer & Seller of Property)

THIS AGREEMENT is made the _____ day of _____ 19_____

Between (1)_____ of _____

_____ (the "Seller");

and

(2)_____ of _____

_____ (the "Buyer").

BACKGROUND

A. The parties have, subject to contract, agreed to a transaction ("the Sale") in which the Seller will sell and the Buyer will buy the property described in the First Schedule ("the Property") at the price of _____ (£_____).

B. The solicitors specified in the Second Schedule ("the Seller's Solicitors") will act for the Seller on the Sale.

C. The solicitors specified in the Third Schedule ("the Buyer's Solicitors") will act for the Buyer on the Sale.

NOW IT IS HEREBY AGREED as follows:

1. EXCLUSIVITY PERIOD

    1.1 The Exclusivity Period shall begin on the exchange of this Agreement and shall end (subject to Clause 5.1 below) at 5 pm on the _____ day after the Buyer's Solicitors receive the draft contract from the Seller's Solicitors pursuant to Clause 2(b) below.

    1.2 If and for as long as the Buyer complies with his obligations under this Agreement, the Seller agrees that during the Exclusivity Period neither the Seller nor anyone acting on the Seller's behalf will:

    (a) seek purchasers for the Property;

    (b) allow any prospective purchaser or mortgagee or any surveyor, valuer or other person acting on his or their behalf to enter the Property (other than under clause 4.3 below);

    (c) provide a draft contract or property information concerning the Property to anyone other than the Buyer's Solicitors;

    (d) negotiate or agree with anyone other than the Buyer or the Buyer's Solicitors any terms for the sale of the Property;

    (e) enter into a commitment to proceed with any other purchaser immediately after the expiry of the Exclusivity Period.

2. SELLER'S INSTRUCTIONS TO SOLICITORS

    The Seller will immediately:

    (a) appoint the Seller's Solicitors to act for him on the Sale; and

    (b) instruct them to send to the Buyer's Solicitors as soon as practicable a draft contract for the Sale and such information about the Property as accords with good conveyancing practice and to deal promptly and reasonably with any enquiries asked by the Buyer's Solicitors and with any amendments to the draft contract proposed by the Buyer's Solicitors.

3. BUYER'S INSTRUCTIONS TO SOLICITORS

    The Buyer will immediately:

    (a) appoint the Buyer's Solicitors to act for him on the Sale; and

    (b) instruct them to make all necessary searches and enquiries as soon as practicable and to deal promptly and in accordance with good conveyancing practice with the draft contract for the Sale and such title and other information about the Property as they receive from the Seller's Solicitors and to negotiate with the Seller's Solicitors promptly and reasonably any amendments to the draft contract which the Buyer's Solicitors propose.

4. SURVEYS, MORTGAGES, ETC.

4.1 If the Buyer requires a mortgage loan in connection with the purchase of the Property, the Buyer shall within _____ week(s) from the date of this Agreement apply to such building society, bank or other prospective lender ("the Mortgagee") as may reasonably be expected to lend the required amount to the Buyer and the Buyer shall complete such application forms and pay such fees as the Mortgagee shall require in order to process the Buyer's application as quickly as possible.

4.2 If the Buyer or the Mortgagee require the Property to be surveyed and/or valued, the Buyer will use all reasonable endeavours to arrange for the survey and/or valuation inspection to take place within _____ days of the date of this Agreement.

4.3 The Seller will give such access to the Property as is reasonably required by any surveyor or valuer appointed by the Buyer or the Mortgagee for the purpose of surveying and/or valuing the Property.

5. GOOD FAITH AND WITHDRAWAL

5.1 During the Exclusivity Period the Seller and the Buyer will deal with each other in good faith and in particular (but without limiting the above):

   (a) if during the Exclusivity Period the Buyer decides not to buy the Property or becomes unable to buy the Property, he will immediately give written notice to that effect to the Seller and the Exclusivity Period will then cease;

   (b) if during the Exclusivity Period the Seller decides not to proceed with the Sale or becomes unable to sell the Property, he will immediately give written notice to that effect to the Buyer and the Buyer's obligations under this Agreement will cease but the restrictions imposed on the Seller by Clause 1.2 above shall continue until the expiry of the Exclusivity Period.

5.2 Nothing in Clause 5.1 above or elsewhere in this Agreement will impose on the Seller any greater duty to disclose matters affecting the Property than are imposed by statute or common law.

6. MISCELLANEOUS

6.1 This Agreement does not bind the parties to the Sale.

6.2 This Agreement does not form part of any other contract.

6.3 In this Agreement the expression "property information" includes title details and any other information about the Property which a prudent prospective buyer or his solicitors would require the seller or his solicitors to provide.

6.4 The headings shall not affect the interpretation of this Agreement.

THE FIRST SCHEDULE — The Property

_____
_____
_____

THE SECOND SCHEDULE — The Seller's Solicitors

_____
_____
_____

THE THIRD SCHEDULE — The Buyer's Solicitors

_____
_____
_____

SIGNED _____   SIGNED _____
by or on behalf of the Seller   by or on behalf of the Buyer

10

ARBITRATION SETTLEMENT OFFER

Date _____

To _____

_____

_____

Ref _____

Dear _____

I am sorry that we seem to be unable to reconcile our differing points of view on_____. I am sure that neither of us wishes to resort to the courts and I therefore suggest that we refer the dispute between us to arbitration. I propose:

1. The dispute be referred to arbitration.

2. The arbitrator shall be _____, who is an expert in these matters. If you cannot agree to him, the arbitrator shall be appointed by the President or Vice-President of the Chartered Institute of Arbitrators.

3. The Rules of the Chartered Institute of Arbitrators in a domestic arbitration shall apply.

4. The costs of the arbitration shall be left to the discretion of the arbitrator.

5. Only one expert witness shall be allowed for each side.

6. The arbitration shall take place at _____and the dispute shall be decided in accordance with English law.

7. The making of an award by the arbitrator shall be a condition precedent to any right of action by either of us against the other in respect of the matter in dispute.

If you agree to this suggestion, please sign and return the enclosed copy of this letter.

Yours sincerely

_____

Name _____

Address _____

_____

Tel. _____

ASSIGNMENT OF MONEY DUE

THIS AGREEMENT is made the _____ day of _____ 19_____

BETWEEN:

(1) _____ of _____ (the "Assignor"); and

(2) _____ of _____ (the "Assignee").

WHEREAS:

(A) The Assignor is entitled to the payment of certain monies under a contract dated _____ 19_____ and made between the Assignor and_____ _____ (the "Contract").

(B) The Assignor wishes to assign the benefit of the Contract to the Assignee.

NOW IT IS HEREBY AGREED as follows:

1.   In consideration for the sum of £_____, receipt of which the Assignor hereby acknowledges, the Assignor assigns and transfers to the Assignee all monies now due and payable to the Assignor and to become due and payable to the Assignor under the terms of the Contract to the Assignee.

2.   The Assignor hereby warrants that there has been no breach of the Contract by any party, and that the Assignor is in full compliance with all the terms and conditions of the Contract, and has not assigned or encumbered all or any rights under said contract.

3.   The Assignor authorises and directs _____ to deliver any and all cheques, drafts, or payments to be issued pursuant to Contract to the Assignee; and further authorises the Assignee to receive such cheques, drafts, or payments from, and to collect any and all funds due or to become due pursuant thereto.

IN WITNESS OF WHICH the parties have signed this agreement the day and year first above written.

_____   _____
Signed by or on behalf of the Assignor   Signed by or on behalf of the Assignee

_____   _____
in the presence of (witness)   in the presence of (witness)

Name _____   Name _____

Address _____   Address _____

_____   _____
Occupation   Occupation

BANK CARD TRANSACTION COMPLAINT

Date _____

To The Manager

             Bank

_____

_____

Ref _____

Dear _____

I am writing regarding an unauthorised [cashpoint][debit card] transaction on my account no._____ which appears on my statement of _____.

As I was _____ at the time of the supposed transaction and could not have made it myself. I have neither written down my PIN number, nor given it to anyone, nor lent my card and I have no reason to believe it has fallen into the wrong hands. Please review my account and confirm that I am not liable for the amount debited.

I look forward to receiving an adjusted statement within 10 days.

Yours sincerely

_____

Name _____

Address _____

_____

Tel. _____

BANK: CHEQUE BOUNCING COMPLAINT

Date _____

To _____ Bank

_____

_____

Ref A/C No. _____

Dear _____

On _____ I paid £_____ to _____ by cheque, number _____ drawn on the above account. I have just been advised by the payee that this cheque has been dishonoured by you.

You will see from your records that I always keep my account in credit and that you have made an error in failing to pay this cheque. This has caused me great embarrassment and inconvenience as this creditor now insists that I pay in cash.

I am also concerned that details of this incident may have been passed to a credit reference agency and that this record may then prejudice my chances of obtaining credit in the future; I am checking whether such a record has been entered.

If it appears that your error leads to my difficulty in obtaining credit I will take legal advice on the amount of damages I should claim from you.

Yours sincerely

Name _____

Address _____

_____

Tel. _____

BANK DISPUTE: OMBUDSMAN INTERVENTION REQUEST

Date _____

To The Banking Ombudsman

70 Gray's Inn Road

London WC1X 8NB

Ref _____

Dear Sir

I am writing because I am in ongoing dispute with the _____ branch
of _____ bank over the following issue:

_____

_____.

I have pursued my claim as far as the bank's headquarters and have used their complaints procedure exhaustively, but without satisfaction. I now request that you intercede on my behalf
and enclose all the relevant documentation.

I look forward to your response.

Yours faithfully

_____

Name _____

Address _____

_____

Tel. _____

BREACH OF CONTRACT NOTICE

Date _____

To _____

_____

_____

Ref _____

Dear _____

We refer to the agreement between us dated _____ 19 _____, which provides that:

_____

_____

_____

PLEASE TAKE NOTE that you are in breach of your obligations under the agreement as follows:

_____

_____

_____

We invite you to remedy the breach by immediately taking steps to do the following:

_____

_____

_____

If you fail to remedy the breach as requested within 14 days of the date of this letter, we shall have no alternative but to commence legal proceedings to claim damages from you as a result of the breach. We will also hold you liable for the costs of those proceedings.

Yours sincerely

Name _____

Address _____

_____

Tel. _____

BREACH OF TENANT'S COVENANTS

Date _____

Ref _____

To _____

_____

_____

Dear Tenant(s),

WITHOUT PREJUDICE

Re. _____

Your tenancy of the above property requires you to comply with a number of obligations such as payment of the rent, repair of the property, etc.

It has come to my/our attention that you have failed to comply as referred to in the Details of Breach(es) below and we ask that you attend to and rectify this situation within a reasonable time failing which I/we will be obliged to pursue our rights against you under the tenancy (including a claim against you for compensation in money for the breach).

Yours faithfully

_____

_____

DETAILS OF BREACH(ES) _____

_____

_____

_____

_____

_____

BUILDERS' WORK COMPLAINT

Date _____

To _____

_____

_____

Ref Estimate No. _____

Dear _____

You carried out building work at the following address _____
as per the above estimate finishing on _____. I am writing to inform you that the work
has proved to be defective in the following manner:

_____

_____

_____

The Supply of Goods and Services Act 1982 requires that should have completed the work
with reasonable skill and care using materials of suitable quality. The defects described above
clearly indicate that have not fulfilled your legal obligations and that you are in breach of contract.

While reserving my rights, I am giving you the opportunity to carry out remedial repairs free
of charge. Failing that I will obtain quotations from other builders and will have them carry
out the work, claiming any expenses incurred from you as I am entitled to do by law.

I look forward to hearing from you within seven days.

Yours sincerely

_____

Name _____

Address _____

_____

Tel. _____

BUILDER/DECORATOR CONTRACT

DATED _____

BETWEEN   **(1)** _____ of _____

_____ (the "Employer");

     and

   (2) _____ of _____

_____ (the "Contractor").

NOW IT IS HEREBY AGREED :

1. The Contractor shall carry out the Works as defined below ("the Works").

2. The Works shall be _____

_____

_____

_____

_____

_____

_____

_____

Any plans or specifications that form part of the description of the Works are attached, have been signed by both parties and form part of this Contract.

3. The Works shall be carried out at _____

_____("the Site") under the direction of _____.

4. The Employer shall pay to the Contractor for the Works £_____ payable as follows:

_____

_____.

5. The Contractor shall begin the Works on or before _____ and shall complete the Works on or before _____ (the "Completion Date"). If the Works have not been completed by the Completion Date the Contractor shall pay or allow to the Employer £_____ per _____ for every_____ or part_____ between the Completion Date and the date of actual completion. The Contractor shall not, however, be responsible for delays outside his control and not reasonably foreseeable by him.

6. The_____ shall obtain every licence, permission or authority required for the exercise of the Works and the _____ shall pay all the fees or charges in respect of them.

7. In carrying out the Works, the Contractor shall use all reasonable skill, care and diligence, suitable good quality materials and comply with any higher specifications of materials or workmanship contained in the description of the Works.

8. The Contractor shall take all reasonable precautions to minimise disruption and the risk of any loss or damage at the Site arising out of the execution of the Works. On completion of the Works the Contractor shall leave the Site clean and tidy to the reasonable satisfaction of the Employer and shall make good at his own cost all damage caused by execution of the Works.

9. The Contractor shall promptly make good any defects or faults which appear within six months of the date of actual completion and are due to materials or workmanship not being in accordance with this Contract entirely at his own cost.

10. The Contractor shall be responsible for any loss or damage to the Site and any death or personal injury arising out of the execution of the Works, confirms that he has or will obtain adequate insurance against any liability and will produce evidence of it to the Employer on request. The Works shall be at the Contractor's risk until Completion.

IN WITNESS OF WHICH the parties hereto have signed this Agreement the day and year first above written.

SIGNED _____ _____
Signed by or on behalf of the Contractor   in the presence of (witness)

Name _____

DATED _____ Address _____

_____

SIGNED _____ _____
Signed by the Employer   in the presence of (witness)

Name _____

DATED _____ Address _____

_____

BUILDING SITE NOISE COMPLAINT

Date _____

To _____

_____

_____

Ref _____

Dear Sirs _____

I am writing to complain about the intolerable level of noise coming from your firm's building site at the following address _____.

I have repeatedly asked your site manager, Mr _____, to reduce the noise but there has been no reduction in it whatsoever. As you are no doubt aware, Section 60 of the 1974 Control of Pollution Act gives local authorities extensive powers of control not only over the hours at which building work can be carried out and the type of machinery used, but also over the level of noise permitted.

If the noise levels are not reduced in the next few days I will have no alternative but to complain to the local environmental health officer.

Yours faithfully

_____

Name _____

Address _____

_____

Tel. _____

CANCELLATION OF AN ORDER TO STOP A CHEQUE

Date _____

_____

_____

_____

Ref _____

Dear _____

On _____ 19 _____, we requested you to stop payment on the following cheque that we issued:

Cheque No: _____

Dated: _____

Amount: _____

Payable to: _____

Account No: _____

We have now advised the payee to re-present the cheque for payment, and we should be grateful if you would now honour the cheque on re-presentation.

Yours sincerely

_____

Account _____

Account No. _____

22

CHILD GUARDIANSHIP CONSENT FORM

I _____, of _____

_____, hereby appoint _____,

of _____, _____, as the

legal guardian of my child(ren). The guardian shall have the following powers:

_____

_____

_____

_____

_____

_____

_____

_____

_____

_____

_____

_____

Signed this _____ day of _____, 19 _____.

_____

_____

23

COHABITATION AGREEMENT
(for Unmarried Partners)

THIS DEED OF AGREEMENT is made the _____ day of _____ 199__

BETWEEN:

(1) _____ of _____ ("the First Party"); and

(2) _____ of _____ ("the Second Party").

WHEREAS:

(a) The Parties live together and wish to enter this Agreement to set out their rights and responsibilities towards each other.

(b) The Parties intend that this Agreement will be legally binding on them.

(c) Each Party enters this Agreement freely and voluntarily and without coercion or pressure from the other Party or anyone else.

1. OWNERSHIP OF THE HOME

The Parties live at the address given above ("the Home") which is a property purchased in their joint names/ in the sole name of the First/Second Party*.

(*delete as appropriate)

2. DIVISION OF PROCEEDS OF SALE OF THE HOME

Where the Home is owned in joint names:

Option 1: The rights and interests of the Parties in the Home and its net proceeds of sale are set out in a Declaration of Trust dated _____ and are not in any way varied or affected by this Deed.

Option 2: The Parties agree that they shall hold the beneficial interest in the Home as tenants in common; in equal shares.

OR

as to _____ % for the First Party and as to _____ % for the Second Party.

OR

in the proportions in which they contribute to the purchase of the Home whether by contribution to the purchase price, payment of mortgage instalments and mortgage-linked endowment premiums, or by way of improvements which add to the value of the Home (and if the Parties cannot agree the value of any such improvements the value shall be determined by a valuer appointed by the President of the Royal Institution of Chartered Surveyors).

Where the Home is owned in the sole name of one Party:

Option 3: The Parties agree that they shall hold the beneficial interest in the Home; in equal shares.

OR

as to _____ % for the First Party and as to _____ % for the Second Party.

OR

in the proportions in which they contribute to the purchase of the Home whether by contribution to the purchase price, payment of mortgage instalments and mortgage-linked endowment premiums, or by way of improvements which add to the value of the Home (and if the Parties cannot agree the value of any such improvements the value shall be determined by a valuer appointed by the President of the Royal Institution of Chartered Surveyors).

24

Option 4: The Parties agree that the First/Second* Party is the sole beneficial owner of the Home and that regardless of contributions to the purchase maintenance or improvement of the Home the other Party is not and will not acquire any beneficial interest in the Home or in its proceeds of sale. _(*delete as appropriate)

3. CONTENTS AND PERSONAL BELONGINGS

Any household and personal item shall be owned:

Option 1: By the Party who acquired it alone (whether by inheritance, gift, purchase or otherwise).

Option 2: By both Parties equally (regardless of when or by whom it was acquired) unless the Parties expressly agree otherwise in writing. Unless the Parties shall agree otherwise within one month of the date of termination of this Agreement all jointly owned items shall be sold and the net proceeds of sale divided equally between them.

4. BANK OR BUILDING SOCIETY ACCOUNTS

It is agreed that:

Option 1: The Parties do not intend to open a joint account. Each Party shall maintain separate bank or building society accounts and the money in each account will remain his or her separate property.

Option 2: The Parties shall maintain a joint bank or building society account ("The Joint Account").

The Parties shall pay into the Joint Account sums sufficient to meet their agreed share of common expenses (referred to in clause 5). The money in the Joint Account shall belong to the Parties in equal shares regardless of the actual sums which either of them may have paid into or withdrawn from the Joint Account. Any money in any bank or building society account maintained separately by either Party shall belong to that Party alone.

5. COMMON EXPENSES

Common household expenditure including mortgage repayments, mortgage-linked endowment premiums, ground rent, service charges, rental payments, buildings and household insurance premiums, council or other local taxes, charges for water rates, gas, electricity, telephone, television licence and rental, food, decoration and repairs shall be:

Option 1: paid by the First/Second* Party alone.

Option 2: shared equally by the Parties.

Option 3: paid as to _____ % by the first Party and as to _____ % by the Second Party.

6. VARIATION/TERMINATION

This Agreement shall be varied only by written agreement of the Parties. This Agreement shall terminate by written agreement of the Parties or upon the death or marriage of either one of them or upon the Parties separation for a period exceeding three months following which the Home shall be valued and either sold and the proceeds divided or the Party leaving compensated appropriately in accordance with the provisions of this Agreement.

SIGNED AS A DEED   **SIGNED AS A DEED**

by the said_____   by the said_____

Name_____   Name_____

in the presence of   in the presence of

Signature_____   Signature_____

Name_____   Name_____

Address_____   Address_____

NOTE: OPTION CLAUSES SHOULD BE DELETED AS APPROPRIATE AND BOTH PARTIES SHOULD INITIAL THE DELETION

COMPANY LET
(for a Furnished or Unfurnished House or Flat)

The PROPERTY _____

_____

The LANDLORD _____

_____

_____

The TENANT _____LIMITED/PLC

whose Registered Office is at_____

_____

_____

_____(Company Registration No._____)

The TERM _____ months beginning on _____

Subject to the right for either party at any time during the Term to end this Agreement
earlier by giving to the other written notice of _____ week(s)/month(s)*

The RENT £ _____ per week/month* payable in advance on the _____ of each week/month*

The DEPOSIT £ _____

The INVENTORY means the list of the Landlord's possessions at the Property which has been signed by the
Landlord and the Tenant

DATED _____

SIGNED _____   _____

_____   _____

(The Landlord)   (Director for and on
                                            behalf of The Tenant)

THIS AGREEMENT comprises the particulars detailed above and the terms and conditions printed overleaf
whereby the Property is hereby let by the Landlord and taken by the Tenant for the Term at the Rent.

Terms and Conditions on next page

Company Let Terms and Conditions

1. The Tenant will:

1.1 pay the Rent at the times and in the manner aforesaid without any deduction abatement or set-off whatsoever

1.2 pay all charges in respect of any electric, gas, water and telephonic or televisual services used at or supplied to the Property and Council Tax or any similar tax that might be charged in addition to or replacement of it

1.3 keep the interior of the Property in a good, clean and tenantable state and condition and not damage or injure the Property or any part of it

1.4 yield up the Property at the end of the Term in the same clean state and condition it was in at the beginning of the Term and if any item listed on the Inventory requires repair, replacing, cleaning or laundering pay for the same (fair wear and tear and damage by insured risks excepted)

1.5 maintain at the Property and keep in a good and clean condition all of the items listed in the Inventory

1.6 not make any alteration or addition to the Property nor without the Landlord's prior written consent to do any redecoration or painting of the Property

1.7 not do or omit to do anything on or at the Property which may be or become a nuisance or annoyance to the Landlord or owners or occupiers of adjoining or nearby premises or which may in any way prejudice the insurance of the Property or cause an increase in the premium payable therefor

1.8 not without the Landlord's prior consent allow or keep any pet or any kind of animal at the Property

1.9 not use or occupy the Property in any way whatsoever other than as a private residence

1.10 not assign, sublet, charge or part with or share possession of occupation of the Property or any part thereof provided however that the Tenant may permit the residential occupation of the Property as a whole by the Tenant's officers and employees, so long as the Tenant continues to be responsible for the Rent and all other outgoings and does not make any charge whatsoever in respect of the same to the occupier and no relationship of landlord and tenant is created or allowed to arise between the tenant and the occupier and provided further that the Landlord's prior written consent (not to be unreasonably withheld) is obtained to each such occupier

1.11 permit the Landlord or anyone authorised by the Landlord at reasonable hours in the daytime and upon reasonable prior notice (except in emergency) to enter and view the Property for any proper purpose (including the checking of compliance with the Tenant's obligations under this Agreement and during the last month of the Term the showing of the Property to prospective new tenants)

1.12 pay interest at the rate of 4% above the Base Lending Rate for the time being of the Landlord's bankers upon any Rent or other money due from the Tenant under this Agreement which is more than 3 days in arrear in respect of the period from when it became due to the date of payment

2. Subject to the Tenant paying the rent and performing his/her obligations under this Agreement the Tenant may peaceably hold and enjoy the Property during the term without interruption from the Landlord or any person rightfully claiming under or in trust for the Landlord

3. The Landlord will:

3.1 insure the property and the items listed on the Inventory

3.2 keep in repair the structure and exterior of the Property (including drains gutters and external pipes)

3.3 keep in repair and proper working order the installations at the Property for the supply of water, gas and electricity and for sanitation (including basins, sinks, baths and sanitary conveniences)

3.3 keep in repair and proper working order the installation at the Property for space heating and heating water

But the Landlord will not be required to:

3.4 carry out works for which the Tenant is responsible by virtue of his/her duty to use the Property in a tenant-like manner

3.5 rebuild or reinstate the Property in the case of destruction or damage by fire or by tempest flood or other inevitable accident

4. In the event of the Rent being unpaid for more than 10 days after it is due (whether demanded or not) or there being a breach of any other of the Tenant's obligations under this Agreement or the Tenant entering into liquidation or having a receiver or administrative receiver appointed then the Landlord may re-enter the Property and this Agreement shall thereupon determine absolutely but without prejudice to any of the Landlord's other rights and remedies in respect of any outstanding obligations on the part of the Tenant

5. The Deposit has been paid by the Tenant and is held by the. Landlord to secure compliance with the Tenant's obligations under this Agreement (without prejudice to the Landlord's other rights and remedies) and if, at any time during the Term, the Landlord is obliged to draw upon it to satisfy any outstanding breaches of such obligations then the Tenant shall forthwith make such additional payment as is necessary to restore the full amount of the Deposit held by the Landlord. As soon as reasonably practicable following termination of this Agreement the Landlord shall return to the Tenant the Deposit or the balance thereof after any deductions properly made

6. The Landlord hereby notifies the Tenant under Section 48 of the Landlord & Tenant Act 1987 that any notices (including notices in proceedings) should be served upon the Landlord at the address stated with the name of the Landlord overleaf

7. In the event of damage to or destruction of the Property by any of the risks insured against by the Landlord the Tenant shall be relieved from payment of the Rent to the extent that the Tenant's use and enjoyment of the Property is thereby prevented and from performance of its obligations as to the state and condition of the Property to the extent of and so long as there prevails such damage or destruction (except to the extent that the insurance is prejudiced by any act or default of the Tenant)

8. So long as the reference to a right of early termination in the definition of the "TERM" overleaf (the "early termination right") has not been deleted then either party may at any time during the Term terminate this Agreement by giving to the other prior written notice to that effect, the length of such notice to be that stated in the early termination right, and upon the expiry of said notice this Agreement shall end with no further liability of either party save for any antecedent breach

9. Where the context so admits:

9.1 The "Landlord" includes the persons for the time being entitled to the reversion expectant upon this Tenancy

9.2 The "Tenant" includes any persons deriving title under the Tenant

9.3 The "Property" includes all of the Landlord's fixtures and fittings at or upon the Property

9.4 The "Term" shall mean the period stated in the particulars overleaf or any shorter or longer period in the event of an earlier termination or an extension or holding over respectively

10. All references to the singular shall include the plural and vice versa and any obligations or liabilities of more than one person shall be joint and several and an obligation on the part of a party shall include an obligation not to allow or permit the breach of that obligation

CONSERVATION AREA TREE ENQUIRY

Date _____

To Planning & Conservation Dept

                  Local Authority

_____ Local Authority

_____

Dear Sirs

Under the terms of the 1990 Town & Country Planning Act I understand any tree in a conservation area which grows on private land is protected, and that your permission must be obtained before cutting it in any way, unless it is dead or dangerous.

I would like to [cut back][uproot] the _____ tree which grows in my [front][back] garden at the below address for the following reason:_____, and as this is a conservation area I am applying for your consent to do this.

I look forward to hearing from you in due course

Yours faithfully

_____

Name _____

Address _____

_____

Tel. _____

CONTRACT AMENDMENT

THIS DEED is made the_____ day of _____ 19 _____

BETWEEN

(1) _____ of _____ (the "First Party"); and

(2) _____ of _____ (the "Second Party").

WHEREAS:

(A) The two parties above have entered into an agreement dated_____19 ___
   (the "Agreement").

(B) The two parties above now wish to vary the terms of the Agreement.

NOW THIS DEED WITNESSES as follows:

1.   The two parties agree that the following additions and amendments to the Agreement shall
apply _____

_____

_____

2.   All other terms and conditions of the Agreement shall remain in full force and effect.

IN WITNESS OF WHICH the parties have executed this deed the day and year first above written.

(Individual)   (Company)

                                                  Signed for and on behalf of
_____
Signed by the First Party
                                                                                  Ltd
_____   _____
in the presence of (witness)

Name   _____
_____   Director
Address
_____
                                                  _____
_____   Director/Secretary
Occupation

                                                  Signed for and on behalf of:
_____
Signed by the Second Party
                                                                                  Ltd
_____   _____
in the presence of (witness)

Name   _____
_____   Director
Address
_____
                                                  _____
_____   Director/Secretary
Occupation

CONTRACT ASSIGNMENT

THIS DEED is made the _____ day of _____ 19_____

BETWEEN:

(1) _____ of _____ (the "Assignor");

(2) _____ of _____ (the "Assignee"); and

(3) _____ of _____ (the "Third Party").

WHEREAS:

(A) The Assignor and the Third Party have entered into an agreement dated_____
_____ 19_____ (the "Agreement").

(B) With the consent of the Third Party the Assignor wishes to assign all its rights and obligations under the Agreement to the Assignee.

NOW THIS DEED WITNESSES as follows:

1.   The Assignor warrants and represents that the Agreement is in full force and effect and is fully assignable.

2.   The Assignee hereby assumes and agrees to perform all the remaining and executory obligations of the Assignor under the Agreement and agrees to indemnify and hold the Assignor harmless from any claim or demand resulting from non-performance by the Assignee.

3.   The Assignee shall be entitled to all monies remaining to be paid under the Agreement, which rights are also assigned hereunder.

4.   The Assignor warrants that the Agreement is without modification, and remains on the terms contained therein.

5.   The Assignor further warrants that it has full right and authority to transfer the Agreement and that the Agreement rights herein transferred are free of lien, encumbrance or adverse claim.

6.   The Third Party agrees to the assignment of the Agreement upon the terms stated herein.

7.   This assignment shall be binding upon and inure to the benefit of the parties, their successors and assigns.

IN WITNESS OF WHICH the parties have executed this deed the day and year first above written.

(Individual)   (Company)

_____   Signed for and on behalf of
Signed by the Assignor

_____   Ltd
in the presence of (witness)   _____
Name
_____
Address   Director
_____   _____

_____   Director/Secretary
Occupation   _____

_____   Signed for and on behalf of:
Signed by the Assignee

_____   Ltd
in the presence of (witness)   _____
Name
_____
Address   Director
_____   _____

_____   Director/Secretary
Occupation   _____

CONTRACTOR/SUBCONTRACTOR AGREEMENT

THIS AGREEMENT is made the _____ day of _____ 19_____,

BETWEEN:

(1) _____ of _____ (the "Contractor"); and

(2) _____ of _____ (the "Subcontractor").

WHEREAS:

(A) The Contractor has entered into an agreement dated _____ 19_____, with _____ (the "Company") for the performance of certain works (the "Works").

(B) The Contractor wishes to subcontract certain portions of the Works to the Subcontractor.

NOW IT IS HEREBY AGREED as follows:

1.   The Subcontractor, as an independent contractor, agrees to furnish all of the labour and materials as may reasonably by required to complete the following portions of the Works:

_____

_____

_____

_____

_____

2.   The Subcontractor agrees that the following portions of the Works will be completed by the dates specified:

Work	Date
_____	_____
_____	_____
_____	_____
_____	_____
_____	_____
_____	_____

3.   The Subcontractor agrees to perform this work in a workmanlike manner according to standard practices. If any plans or specifications are part of this job, they are attached to and form part of this agreement.

4.   The Contractor agrees to pay the Subcontractor £ _____ as payment for the full performance of its obligations hereunder. This sum will be paid to the Subcontractor on satisfactory completion of the work in the following manner and on the following dates:

_____

_____

5.   The Contractor and Subcontractor may agree to extra services and work, but any such extras must be set out and agreed to in writing by both the Contractor and the Subcontractor.

6.   The Subcontractor agrees to indemnify and hold the Contractor harmless from any claims or liability arising from the Subcontractor's work under this Contract.

7.   No modification of this agreement will be effective unless it is in writing and is signed by both parties. This agreement binds and benefits both parties and any successors. Time is of the essence in this agreement. This document, including any attachments is the entire agreement between the parties.

IN WITNESS OF WHICH the parties have signed this agreement the day and year first above written.

_____

Signed by or on behalf of the Contractor

_____

in the presence of (witness)

Name _____

Address _____

_____

Occupation _____

_____

Signed by or on behalf of the Subcontractor

_____

in the presence of (witness)

Name _____

Address _____

_____

Occupation _____

COPYRIGHT MATERIAL LICENCE

THIS LICENCE IS MADE the _____ day of _____ 19 _____

BETWEEN:

(1) _____ of _____ (the "Licensor"); and

(2) _____ of _____ (the "Licensee").

NOW IT IS HEREBY AGREED as follows:

1.   In consideration for the sum of £ _____, receipt of which the Licensor hereby acknowledges, the Licensor grants to the Licensee a licence to use, reprint and publish the following material (the "Copyright Material"):

_____

_____

2.   The Copyright Material shall be used by the Licensee only in the following manner or publication and for the following period:

_____

_____

3.   The Copyright Material shall be used by the Licensee only in the following territory of the world:

_____

_____

4.   The Licensee agrees that the Licensor shall retain the worldwide copyright in the Copyright Material, and the moral rights of the author of the Copyright Material are hereby asserted.

5.   This agreement shall be binding upon and inure to the benefit of the parties, their successor and assigns.

IN WITNESS OF WHICH the parties have agreed this licence the day and year first above written.

_____   _____
Signed by or on behalf of the Licensor   Signed by or on behalf of the Licensee

_____   _____
in the presence of (witness)   in the presence of (witness)

Name _____   Name _____

Address _____   Address _____

_____   _____

Occupation _____   Occupation _____

33

CREDIT ACCOUNT APPLICATION

with _____ Ltd

Company Name	
Address	Invoice Address (if different)
Tel No.	Fax No.

Name of Buyer		
Registration No.	Value of Initial Order £	Requested Credit Limit £
Trade Reference (1)	Trade Reference (2)	Bank Reference

Parent Company (if applicable) _____

I hereby agree to the terms and conditions of sale accompanying this application.

NAME _____

POSITION _____

SIGNED _____ DATE _____

OFFICE USE ONLY

	Date	Agency Rating	Credit Limit	Authorised	Date
Application Rec'd		Accounts Rec'd			
Refs Applied For					
Account Opened					

Account No. [ ]   Credit Limit [ ]

CREDIT CARD COMPANY CLAIM

Date _____

To _____

_____

_____

Ref Card No. _____

Dear _____

On _____ I purchased the following _____, value £_____ supplied by_____, using my _____ credit card, account number _____.

However, the [goods][services] have proved defective for the following reason:_____
_____
_____.

Under the Consumer Credit Act 1974, credit card companies can be held liable by customers for breach of contract if the value of the purchase was over £100. I am holding you in breach of contract and am legally entitled to seek compensation from you as well as from the supplier.

Please contact me within 10 days so I can pursue my claim.

Yours sincerely

_____

Name _____

Address _____

_____

Tel _____

CREDIT COMPANY: REFERENCE AGENCY NAME REQUEST

Date _____

To _____

_____

_____

Dear _____

Loan application reference_____

I refer to my recent application for a loan. I am now exercising my rights under section 157 of the Consumer Credit Act 1974. Would you please let me have details of any credit reference agency you approached for information about me.

I look forward to hearing from you within seven working days of your receiving this letter.

Yours sincerely

_____

Name _____

Address _____

_____

Tel. _____

CREDIT REFERENCE AGENCY: FILE REQUEST

Date _____

To _____

_____

_____

Dear Sirs

I would like to exercise my rights under section 158(1) of the Consumer Credit Act 1974. I enclose a postal order for £1 and request a copy of my file.

I have been living at the above address for ___ years. Before that I lived at _____

_____ [I am sometimes known by my middle name

of _____] [I have my own business which trades under the name of _____

and uses my home address].

I look forward to hearing from you within seven working days of receiving this letter.

Yours faithfully

_____

Name _____

Address _____

_____

Tel. _____

CREDIT REFERENCE AGENCY:
FURTHER INFO. REQUEST FOR A BUSINESS

Date _____

To _____

_____

_____

Dear Sirs

Re my file number_____

Thank you for your letter of _____ and the enclosed extracts from my file. I note that you are dealing with my request for information under section 160 of the Consumer Credit Act 1974.

I have considered the information you sent me and I do not consider that this is sufficient to give me the overall picture of your view of my creditworthiness. I am currently seeking a loan to help me expand my business and I need to know my chances of success before embarking on this project. Would you please therefore let me have a copy of all the information you hold about me.

Yours faithfully

_____

Name _____

Address _____

_____

Tel. _____

CREDIT REFERENCE AGENCY INFO ON A BUSINESS: INTERVENTION OF DIRECTOR OF FAIR TRADING REQUEST

Date _____

To The Director General of Fair Trading

Field House

15-25 Bream's Buildings

London EC4A 1PR

Dear Sir

Application under section 160 of the Consumer Credit Act 1974

I enclose copies of my correspondence with _____ Credit Reference Agency which is dealing with my request for a copy of my file under section 160 of the Consumer Credit Act 1974.

You will see that I am not happy with the information I have been given and I have not been able to resolve the problem with the agency. Would you please now intervene and decide whether I should be allowed fuller information about my file.

Please contact me if you need further information.

Yours faithfully

_____

Name _____

Address _____

_____

Tel. _____

CREDIT REFERENCE AGENCY:
INTERVENTION OF OFFICE OF FAIR TRADING REQUEST

Date _____

To The Director General of Fair Trading

Field House

15-25 Bream's Buildings

London EC4A 1PR

Dear Sir

_____**Credit Reference Agency**

Application under section 159(5) Consumer Credit Act 1974

I enclose copies of all the correspondence between myself and _____
Credit Reference Agency, address _____.

You will see from this that on _____ I asked _____ Credit
Reference Agency to add a Notice of Correction to my file as they had refused to amend or
delete an entry relating to _____.
_____. Credit Reference Agency have now written to inform me that they
are not prepared to add my Notice of Correction to my file.

I should be grateful if you would now intervene in this dispute as I believe my interests will
be severely prejudiced because _____ if this entry remains on my
file without further explanation.

Please contact me if I can provide you with any further information.

Yours faithfully

_____

Name _____

Address _____

_____

Tel. _____

CREDIT REFERENCE AGENCY:
NOTICE OF CORRECTION RE BANKRUPTCY

Date _____

To _____ Credit Reference Agency

_____

_____

Ref _____

Dear Sirs _____

My file (your reference number _____)

Thank you for your letter of _____. I note that you are not prepared to delete the information about my discharged bankruptcy from my file. Would you please therefore add the following Notice of Correction to my file.

Notice of Correction

I _____ of _____ wish to record that the details of the bankruptcy recorded on my file relate to a bankruptcy which was discharged on _____. I was made bankrupt because I was unable to pay a supplier's bill of £_____ under the following circumstances_____
_____
_____. I paid off the £_____ (___months after it was due, as soon as I could). I have not been made bankrupt at any other time. I would ask anyone considering my file to take this Notice of Correction into account.

Would you please let me know, within 28 days of your receiving this letter, whether you have added this Notice of Correction to my file.

Yours faithfully

_____

Name _____

Address _____

_____

CREDIT REFERENCE AGENCY:
PERSONAL FILE COURT JUDGMENT CORRECTION

Date _____

To _____ Credit Reference Agency

_____

_____

Ref _____

Dear Sirs

My file (your reference number _____)

Thank you for your letter of _____ with which you enclosed a copy of my file.

I am writing under section 159(1) of the Consumer Credit Act 1974 to ask you to correct one of the entries. The judgment against me for £_____ was settled on _____.
I enclose a Certificate of Satisfaction from the County Court as proof of this.

I look forward to hearing from you within 28 days of your receiving this letter..

Yours faithfully

_____

Name _____

Address _____

_____

Tel. _____

CREDIT REFERENCE AGENCY:
PERSONAL FILE DISSOCIATION CORRECTION

Date _____

To _____ Credit Reference Agency

_____

_____

Ref _____

Dear Sirs

My file reference number _____

Thank you for your letter of _____ with which you enclosed a copy of my file.

I note that my file contains information about _____, my former partner. _____ has not lived at this address for _____ years and I have no financial connection with him/her. Would you please remove the information about him//her from my file.

Yours faithfully

_____

Name _____

Address _____

_____

Tel. _____

CREDIT REFERENCE AGENCY:
REFERRAL TO DATA PROTECTION AGENCY

Date _____

To The Data Protection Agency
Complaints Dept
Wycliffe House
Water Lane
Wilmslow
Cheshire SK9 5AF

Ref _____

Dear Sirs

I am writing to ask you to resolve my dispute with _____ Credit Reference Agency. I enclose copies of all correspondence which has passed between us.

You will see that _____ Credit Reference Agency does not accept that I have no financial connection with _____, my former partner, and refuses to delete the information about him/her from my file.

Please let me know if you need any further information from me. I look forward to hearing from you.

Yours faithfully

_____

Name _____

Address _____

_____

Tel. _____

CREDIT REFERENCE AGENCY:REQUEST FOR REPORT

Date _____

To _____

_____

_____

Dear Sirs

Re: File No. _____

We request a detailed credit report on the above. They have requested credit terms represent-·
ing a monthly risk to us of approximately £ _____. We enclose our cheque for
£ _____ and would ask you to fax or post your report to us as soon as possible.

Yours sincerely

_____

Name _____

Address _____

_____

Tel. _____

DEBT ACKNOWLEDGEMENT

The undersigned hereby confirms and acknowledges to _____
("the Creditor") that the undersigned is indebted to the Creditor in the amount of £ _____
as of the date hereof, which amount is due and owing and includes all accrued interest and
other permitted charges to date. The undersigned further acknowledges that there are no cred-
its or rights of set off against the balance owing.

Signed this _____ day of _____ 19 _____.

In the presence of

_____   _____
Witness   Debtor

DEBT COLLECTION: SOLICITOR INSTRUCTION

Date _____

To _____

_____

_____

Dear _____

Re _____

Debt £ _____

Please issue proceedings to recover the amount £ _____ from the above named company.

We enclose a copy of our invoice together with our complete file relating to this debt. Please let us know if you require any further information.

No complaint has been received in respect of this debt and all our applications for payment have been ignored. We draw your attention to our last letter in which we gave warning that unless payment was received, proceedings would be commenced without further notice.

We will let you know immediately if any payment is received by us.

Yours sincerely

_____

Name _____

Address _____

_____

Tel. _____

DEFECTIVE GOODS NOTICE

Date _____

To _____

_____

_____

Ref _____

Dear _____

This is to inform you that I have received goods delivered by you as per your invoice or order no. _____, dated _____ 19 _____.

Certain goods as listed on the attached sheet are defective for the following reasons:

_____

_____

_____

Under the amended Sale of Goods Act 1979 you are legally obliged to supply goods that are of satisfactory quality. Accordingly, I wish to return these goods in exchange for a credit note in the amount of £_____. I also intend to return the goods to you at your cost unless you collect them.

Please confirm the credit and also issue instructions for the return of the goods. You are advised by this notice that I reserve my legal rights. I look forward to your prompt reply.

Yours sincerely

_____

Name _____

Address _____

_____

Tel. _____

DEMAND TO ACKNOWLEDGE DELIVERY DATES

Date _____

To _____

_____

_____

Ref _____

Dear _____

We request that you confirm and specify delivery arrangements in respect of my order dated _____ 19 ____, and further confirm that you will abide by those arrangements.

Failure to provide this confirmation shall constitute a breach of contract and I shall no longer consider myself bound by this contract. Further, I shall hold you responsible for all resultant damages as provided by law.

Please confirm delivery dates, in writing, no later than _____ 19 ____.

Yours sincerely

_____

Name _____

Address _____

_____

Tel. _____

DISPUTED ACCOUNT NOTICE

Date _____

To _____

_____

_____

Ref _____

Dear _____

I refer to your invoice/order/statement no. _____, dated _____ 19 ____, in the amount of £_____.

I dispute the balance you claim to be owed for the following reason(s):

_____ Items invoiced for have not been received.

_____ Prices are in excess of the agreed amount. A credit of £ _____ is claimed.

_____ My payment of £ _____ made on _____ 19_____, has not been credited.

_____ Goods delivered to me were not ordered and are available for return on delivery instructions.

_____ Goods were defective as per prior letter.

_____ Goods are available for return and credit as per your sales terms.

_____ Other: _____

Please credit my account promptly in the amount of £_____ so it may be satisfactorily cleared.

Yours sincerely

_____

ELECTRICITY BILL QUERY

Date _____

To _____

_____

_____

Ref _____

Dear _____

I have received my bill reference number _____ dated _____ regarding the above account.

I am writing to question the accuracy of the meter reading, as the units of electricity consumed appear to be far above my normal usage for this time of year. I have tested the meter with all electrical appliances in the property turned off and observed the meter still running. There must either be a leakage to earth or the meter is faulty.

Please therefore arrange for an engineer to test the meter so we can determine its accuracy and settle the matter. Please advise me of any charge for doing this and confirm that costs for meter testing are refundable should the meter indeed prove faulty and that in addition I may be entitled to compensation.

I look forward to hearing from you with a proposed appointment date.

Yours sincerely

_____

Name _____

Address _____

_____

Tel. _____

ELECTRICITY BILL QUERY
OFFER INVESTIGATION REQUEST

Date _____

Office of Electricity Regulation (OFFER)

Hagley House

83-85 Hagley Road

Birmingham B16 8QG

Ref _____

Dear Sirs

I am writing to request your intervention in my dispute with _____ Electricity Company which remains unresolved.

Please refer to the enclosed bills and correspondence relating to this case. As you will see, the amount of bill in dispute does not appear to be in line with previous bills, despite the fact that use of my electrical appliances has remained virtually unchanged. I also tested the meter with all appliances turned off and it was still running. Thus, I have ample reason to believe the meter is no longer accurate.

I should be grateful if you would look into my claim and send an independent Meter Examiner. It is my understanding that during your investigations my services will not be interrupted nor any legal action be taken regarding the non-payment of the bill.

Please keep me informed on the progress of this investigation.

Yours faithfully

_____

Name _____

Address _____

_____

Tel. _____

EMPLOYEE LET
(for a Furnished or Unfurnished House or Flat)

The PROPERTY _____

_____

The LICENSOR _____

_____

_____

The LICENSEE _____

_____

_____

_____

_____

The PERIOD the period beginning on the date of this Agreement and ending on the date that the

Licensee's employment with the Licensor ceases

(delete paragraph if not required) [Subject to the right for either party at any time during the Period to end this Agreement

earlier by giving to the other written notice of _____ week(s)/month(s)*] (* delete as appropriate)

The LICENCE FEE £ _____ per week/month* payable in advance on the _____ of each week/month*

The DEPOSIT £ _____

[**The INVENTORY** means the list of the Licensor's possessions at the Property which has been signed by the (delete if unfurnished)

Licensor and the Licensee]

DATED _____

SIGNED _____   _____

_____   _____

(The Licensor)   (The Licensee)

THIS AGREEMENT comprises the particulars detailed above and the terms and conditions printed overleaf whereby the Property is hereby let by the Licensor and taken by the Licensee for the Period at the Licence Fee.

Terms and Conditions on next page

53

EMPLOYEE LET
Terms and Conditions

1. It is hereby agreed that the Licensor is allowing the Licensee to reside at the property solely in consequence of and in connection with the Licensee's employment with the Licensor and on the termination of such employment this Agreement shall forthwith terminate and, further, that the Licensor may deduct the Licence Fee and any other payments due and outstanding from the Licensee under this Agreement from any wages or salary that may from time to time due from the Licensor to the Licensee

2. The Licensee will:

2.1 pay the Licence Fee at the times and in the manner aforesaid without any deduction abatement or set-off whatsoever

2.2 pay all charges in respect of any electric, gas, water and telephonic or televisual services used at or supplied to the Property and Council Tax or any similar tax that might be charged in addition to or replacement of it

2.3 keep the interior of the property in a good clean and tenantable state and condition and not damage or injure the Property or any part of it and if at the end of the Period any item on the Inventory requires repair, replacing, cleaning or laundering the Licensee will pay for the same (reasonable wear and tear and damage by an insured risk excepted)

2.4 maintain at the Property and keep in a good and clean condition all of the items listed in the Inventory

2.5 not make any alteration or addition to the Property nor without the Licensor's prior written consent to do any redecoration or painting of the Property

2.6 not do or omit to do anything on or at the Property which may be or become a nuisance or annoyance to the Licensor or owners or occupiers of adjoining or nearby premises or which may in any way prejudice the insurance of the Property or cause an increase in the premium payable therefor

2.7 not without the Licensor's prior consent allow or keep any pet or any kind of animal at the Property

2.8 not use or occupy the Property in any way whatsoever other than as a private residence

2.9 not part with or share possession of occupation of the Property or any part thereof provided however that members of the Licensee's immediate family may reside at the Property with the Licensee so long as no relationship of Licensor and Licensee is thereby created or allowed to arise

2.10 permit the Licensor or anyone authorised by the Licensor at reasonable hours in the daytime and upon reasonable prior notice (except in emergency) to enter and view the Property for any proper purpose (including the checking of compliance with the Licensee's obligations under this Agreement and during the last month of the Period the showing of the Property to prospective new licensees)

2.11 pay interest at the rate of 4% above the Base Lending Rate for the time being of the Licensor's bankers upon any Licence Fee or other money due from the Licensee under this Agreement which is more than 3 days in arrear in respect of the period from when it became due to the date of payment

3. In the event of the Licence Fee being unpaid for more than 10 days after it is due (whether demanded or not) or there being a breach of any other of the Licensee's obligations under this Agreement then the Licensor may re-enter the Property and this Agreement shall thereupon determine absolutely but without prejudice to any of the Licensor's other rights and remedies in respect of any outstanding obligations on the part of the Licensee

4. The Deposit has been paid by the Licensee and is held by the Licensor to secure compliance with the Licensee's obligations under this Agreement (without prejudice to the Licensor's other rights and remedies) and if, at any time during the Period, the Licensor is obliged to draw upon it to satisfy any outstanding breaches of such obligations then the Licensee shall forthwith make such additional payment as is necessary to restore the full amount of the Deposit held by the Licensor. As soon as reasonably practicable following termination of this Agreement the Licensor shall return to the Licensee the Deposit or the balance thereof after any deductions properly made

5. The owner will insure the Property and the items listed on the Inventory

6. The Licensor hereby notifies the Licensee under Section 48 of the Licensor & Licensee Act 1987 that any notices (including notices in proceedings) should be served upon the Licensor at the address stated with the name of the Licensor overleaf

7. In the event of damage to or destruction of the Property by any of the risks insured against by the Licensor the Licensee shall be relieved from payment of the Licence Fee to the extent that the Licensee's use and enjoyment of the Property is thereby prevented and from performance of its obligations as to the state and condition of the Property to the extent of and so long as there prevails such damage or destruction (except to the extent that the insurance is prejudiced by any act or default of the Licensee)

8. So long as the reference to a right of early termination in the definition of the "PERIOD" overleaf (the "early termination right") has not been deleted then either party may at any time during the Period terminate this Agreement by giving to the other prior written notice to that effect, the length of such notice to be that stated in the early termination right, and upon the expiry of said notice this Agreement shall end with no further liability of either party save for any antecedent breach

9. Where the context so admits:

8.1 The "Licensor" includes the persons for the time being entitled to the reversion expectant upon this Tenancy

8.2 The "Licensee" includes any persons deriving title under the Licensee

8.3 The "Property" includes all of the Licensor's fixtures and fittings at or upon the Property

8.4 The "Period" shall mean the period stated in the particulars overleaf or any shorter or longer period in the event of an earlier termination or an extension or holding over respectively

10. All references to the singular shall include the plural and vice versa and any obligations or liabilities of more than one person shall be joint and several and an obligation on the part of a party shall include an obligation not to allow or permit the breach of that obligation

EMPLOYMENT REFERENCE REQUEST

Date _____

From _____

_____

_____

To _____

_____

_____

I have applied for a job with _____

        Address _____

_____

        Contact _____

I have been asked to provide references to this potential employer to support my job application.

I should be grateful if you would provide the above company with a written reference of behalf of me, based on your knowledge and experience of my work and character while under your employment.

Thank you in advance for your co-operation.

Yours sincerely

_____

ENVIRONMENAL HEALTH OFFICER HYGIENE COMPLAINT

Date _____

To The Environmental Health Officer

_____ Council

_____

Dear Sir

Re _____

I am writing to ask you to investigate the hygiene conditions of the above [caterer][restaurant][wine bar][pub]. I believe their food safety standards are questionable after several members of my party of ____ suffered from severe food poisoning as a direct result of eating _____ on _____, as verified by our GPs.

I look forward to hearing the result of your investigation

Yours faithfully

_____

Name _____

Address _____

_____

Tel. _____

ESTATE AGENT APPOINTMENT:SOLE AGENCY

Date _____

To _____

_____

_____

Dear _____

Re _____

We hereby instruct you as agents to sell the above-mentioned property at a price of not less than £_____ on a 'sole agency basis', and agree to pay commission of ___% on the purchase amount. [In addition we agree to pay the charges as set out in your letter of _____.]

We reserve the right to withdraw these instructions at any time before you have introduced a purchaser.

We do not intend to appoint any other agent to sell the property for a period of _____ months. If after that time the property remains unsold we reserve the right to withdraw your instruction and appoint another agent if necessary. Should we find a buyer ourselves during this period we are not, under a sole agency basis, obliged to pay your commission.

Yours sincerely

_____

Name _____

Address _____

_____

Tel. _____

ESTATE AGENT APPOINTMENT:SOLE SELLING RIGHTS

Date _____

To _____

_____

_____

Dear _____

Re _____

We hereby instruct you in person to sell the above-mentioned property at a price of not less than £_____ on a 'sole selling rights' basis and agree to pay you commission of ___% on the purchase amount. [In addition, we agree to pay the charges as set out in your letter of _____.]

We reserve the right to withdraw these instructions at any time before you have introduced a purchaser.

We do not intend to appoint any other agent to sell the property for a period of _____ months. If after that time the property remains unsold we reserve the right to withdraw your instruction and appoint another agent if necessary. It is understood that should we find a buyer ourselves during this period we will, under a sole selling rights basis, still pay you your commission.

Yours sincerely

_____

Name _____

Address _____

Tel. _____

EXECUTOR'S LETTER TO DECEASED'S BANK

Date _____

To The Manager

_____ Bank _____

_____

Dear Sir

Re_____, deceased

Account number_____.

I am an executor of the estate of the late _____ who died on_____.
My co-executor is _____ who lives at _____.
I enclose a copy of the death certificate, which I should be grateful if you would return once you have noted the details.

Please would you:

1. Put an immediate stop on all unpaid cheques and standing orders from the above account.

2. Let me know the balance on the account at the date of death and, as a separate figure, any interest accrued but not credited up to that date.

3. Send me a list of any deeds and documents you are holding on _____behalf.

4. Let me know the amount of interest paid during the current tax year up to the date of death, whether it was paid gross or net and the amount of any tax deducted.

My co-executor and I wish to open an executor's account and I should be grateful if you would send me the appropriate forms for us to sign in order to do this.

Yours faithfully

_____

Name _____

Address _____

Tel. _____

EXECUTOR'S LETTER TO DECEASED'S MORTGAGE LENDER

Date _____

To _____

_____

_____

Dear Sirs

I am an executor of the estate of _____, address: _____, roll number_____,who died on _____. My other co-executors are _____ of _____ and _____ of _____. I enclose a copy of the death certificate, which I should be grateful if you would return to me once you have noted the details

Please let me know the amount outstanding on the above mortgage and the amount of interest due at the date of death.

_____ held an endowment policy with _____ reference number _____. Please let me know what sum is payable under the policy following his/her death and if there will be any surplus remaining after repayment.

Yours faithfully

_____

Name _____

Address _____

Tel. _____

EXERCISE OF OPTION

Date _____

To _____

_____

_____

Ref _____

Dear _____

You are hereby notified that I have elected to and hereby exercise and accept the option dated _____ 19 _____, executed by you in my favour. I agree to all terms, conditions, and provisions of the option.

Yours sincerely

_____

Name _____

Address _____

_____

Tel. _____

EXTENSION OF OPTION TO PURCHASE PROPERTY

THIS AGREEMENT IS MADE the _____ day of _____ 19_____

BETWEEN:

(1) _____ (the "Grantor"); and

(2) _____ (the "Holder").

WHEREAS:

(A) The Grantor, as the owner of property located at _____
_____ (the "Property") granted an option to buy the
Property to the Holder on _____ 19_____ (the "Option"), which expires
on _____ 19_____ .

(B) The Holder wished to extend the term of the Option.

NOW IT IS HEREBY AGREED as follows:

1.   In consideration for the payment to Grantor by Holder of the sum of _____
_____Pounds (£_____), the receipt of which is
hereby acknowledged, the Option will be extended and terminate and expire at _____ on
_____19____ .

2.   The extension of the Option upon the payment as set forth above shall be an extension of
the expiration of the Option only and all other terms and conditions in the Option shall remain
in force and effect.

3.   If the Holder exercises the Option before the expiration of the further term herein granted
the payment for the Option and the payment for extension of the expiration of the Option shall
be applied towards the purchase price of the Property and the Holder shall receive a credit on
completion equal to the amount(s) paid for the Option and any extension.

4.   If the Holder fails to exercise the Option before the expiration of the further term herein
agreed the Grantor shall be entitled to return absolutely all payment made by the Holder to the
Grantor for the Option and the extension granted herein.

IN WITNESS OF WHICH the parties have signed this Agreement the day and year first above
written.

_____   _____
Signed by or on behalf of the Grantor   Signed by or on behalf of the Holder

_____   _____
in the presence of (witness)   in the presence of (witness)

Name _____   Name _____

Address _____   Address _____

_____   _____

Occupation _____   Occupation _____

FAMILY TREE

Name: _____

Father: _____   Mother: _____

Father's   **Mother's**

Father: _____   Father: _____

Mother: _____   Mother: _____

Father's Paternal   **Mother's Paternal**

Grandfather: _____   Grandfather: _____

Grandmother: _____   Grandmother: _____

Father's Maternal   **Mother's Maternal**

Grandfather: _____   Grandfather: _____

Grandmother: _____   Grandmother: _____

Paternal Side: Father's Siblings: _____

_____

Your Paternal Cousins: _____

_____

Your Grandfather's Siblings: _____

_____

Your Grandmother's Siblings: _____

_____

Maternal Side: Mother's Siblings: _____

_____

Your Maternal Cousins: _____

_____

Your Grandfather's Siblings: _____

_____

Your Grandmother's Siblings: _____

_____

FINAL NOTICE BEFORE LEGAL PROCEEDINGS

Date _____

To _____

_____

_____

Ref _____

Dear _____

I have repeatedly requested payment of your long-overdue account in the amount of £ _____.

Unless I receive payment in full of this amount within seven days of the date of this letter I shall have no alternative but to refer your account to our solicitors for recovery. This will result in you being liable for further costs.

Yours sincerely

_____

Name _____

Address _____

_____

Tel. _____

FOOTBALL POOLS SYNDICATE AGREEMENT

For the Football Pools competition run by: _____

and called: _____

SYNDICATE NAME: _____

MANAGER	DATE OF APPOINTMENT	SIGNATURE

MEMBER	INDIVIDUAL STAKE (to be paid IN ADVANCE of each Match Day by the agreed deadline)	DATE JOINED SYNDICATE	MANAGER'S SIGNATURE	MEMBER'S SIGNATURE	DATE LEFT SYNDICATE	MANAGER'S SIGNATURE

Agreed deadline for payment of Individual Stakes: Time: _____

Day: _____ **days before each Match Day**

Syndicate Rules on next page

FOOTBALL POOLS SYNDICATE RULES

1. Definitions

'**Coupon**' means an appropriate coupon or coupons for the agreed pools competition;

'**Individual Stake**' means the stake payable by each Member as set out in this Agreement and received by the Manager in advance of each Match Day before the agreed deadline;

'**Manager**' means the Manager of the Syndicate, who shall be appointed and may be replaced at any time without notice by a majority of the Members;

'**Match Day**' means a day or days of scheduled football matches for which a Coupon may be submitted under the agreed pools competition;

'**Members**' means all those persons who have joined and not left the Syndicate;

'**Syndicate Stake**' means the total of the Members' Individual Stakes in respect of any Match Day.

2. Manager's Responsibilities

2.1 The Manager will:

(**a**) establish a procedure for agreeing the match selections to be entered by the Syndicate for each Match Day;

(**b**) complete and enter a Coupon bearing the agreed match selections for the amount of the Syndicate Stake for each Match Day. However, if the Syndicate Stake is not sufficient to buy a Coupon bearing all agreed match selections for any Match Day, the Manager shall have absolute discretion as to which of the match selections to enter;

(**c**) collect any prize money and account to the Members for it in proportion to their Individual Stakes, holding it in trust for the Members in the meantime.

2.2 If any Member fails to pay his or her Individual Stake to the Manager in advance of any Match Day by the agreed deadline, the Manager may (but shall not be obliged to) pay that Individual Stake on the Member's behalf and, if the Manager does so, the Member will reimburse the Manager forthwith upon demand.

2.3 The Manager shall not be liable to any Member for any loss or damage arising out of any failing of the Manager under this Agreement, provided that the Manager has acted honestly.

3. Member's Responsibilities

The Members will each pay their Individual Stake to the Manager in advance of each Match Day by the agreed deadline.

4. Ceasing to be a Member

A Member shall be removed from the Group:

4.1 if the Member wishes to leave; or

4.2 at the discretion of the Manager, if the Member fails to pay his or her Individual Stake in accordance with Rule 3 in respect of any 3 weeks (whether consecutive or non-consecutive); or

4.3 at the discretion of the Manager, if the Member fails to reimburse the Manager in accordance with Rule 2.2.

5. This Agreement

5.1 It shall be the responsibility of the Manager to update and amend this Agreement. Any such amendment, other than the removal of a Member in accordance with Rule 4, must have been authorised by majority vote of the Members.

5.2 The list of Members in this Agreement shall be conclusive as to the membership of the Syndicate at any point in time, provided that a person whose application for membership has been accepted by the Manager and who has duly paid an agreed Individual Stake shall not be excluded from a share of prize money under Rule 2.1(c) merely because the Agreement has not been updated to record that person as a Member.

5.3 The appointment or replacement of the Manager shall take effect whether or not this Agreement has been amended to that effect.

FUNERAL INSTRUCTIONS

OF

_____
(NAME)

**FUNERAL
(BURIAL/CREMATION)** _____

_____

UNDERTAKER _____

_____

**PLACE OF
SERVICE** _____

_____

**TYPE OF
SERVICE** _____

_____

**PERSON
OFFICIATING** _____

_____

**MUSIC
SELECTION** _____

_____

**READING
SELECTION** _____

_____

FLOWERS _____

_____

**SPECIAL
INSTRUCTIONS** _____

_____

_____

_____

GARAGE SERVICE BILL COMPLAINT

Date _____

To _____

_____

_____

Dear _____

On _____ I bought in my _____ registration number_____ for repairs which your reception mechanic estimated would cost £_____. However, when I came to pick the car up on _____ I was dismayed at being presented with a bill for £_____. I had to pay the bill in order to drive the car away, but did so express-ly under protest, saying I would take the matter up in writing.

Although we had not agreed a set price for the work I am by law only obliged to pay a rea-sonable price for your services. Judging by your initial estimate and also by the enclosed copies of estimates I have since obtained from [other garages][the RAC][the AA] of £_____ and £_____ for the same work, I am exercising my rights under law by rejecting your bill as unreasonably high.

I estimate that the work done on my car was worth £_____, taking into consideration your original estimate and the others I have obtained, but no more. Please therefore send me a cheque for £_____, representing the amount you overcharged me within 10 days.

I look forward to hearing from you.

Yours sincerely

Name _____

Address _____

_____

Tel. _____

GARAGE SERVICE CLAIM

Date _____

To _____

_____

_____

_____

Dear _____

Re Model _____ Reg. No._____

On _____ I brought in the above vehicle for [a full service][repairs to _____]. I was subsequently informed that the following needed attention _____ and agreed to have the necessary work carried out. On picking up the car on _____ I paid the bill for £_____ in full and received a schedule of the parts tested and work carried out.

However, on _____, just _____ days after it was returned to me, the vehicle developed the following problems _____ which should not have arisen after [a full service][the above repairs]. I had to have the defect remedied at a cost of £_____, as evidenced by the enclosed receipt.

Under the Supply of Goods and Services Act of 1982, you are responsible for supplying quality goods and satisfactory service. Your failure to return my car in satisfactory condition constitutes your breach of contract and you are liable for the expenses I incurred in having the car repaired.

Please send me a cheque for this sum within 10 days. Otherwise, I shall have no alternative but to issue you a county court summons for recovery of the amount owed to me without further notice.

Yours sincerely

Name _____

Address _____

_____

Tel. _____

GAS BILL QUERY

Date _____

To _____

_____

_____

Ref _____

Dear _____

I have received my bill dated _____ regarding the above account.

The amount of the bill appears to be far above my normal usage for this time of year. I can only think that either the gas meter is faulty or you have made a billing error.

Please respond with an appropriate adjustment on the bill or a proposed date for an engineer to come and test the meter.

Yours sincerely

Name _____

Address _____

_____

Tel. _____

GAS COMPLAINT:
GCC INVESTIGATION REQUEST

Date _____

Gas Consumers Council

Abford House

15 Wilton Road

London SW1V 1LT

Ref _____

Dear Sirs

I am writing regarding my dispute with _____ gas company which has yet to be resolved.

Please refer to the enclosed bills and correspondence relating to this case which concerns :

_____

_____.

I should be grateful if you would please look into this case on my behalf. I understand that during your investigation my gas supply will not be interrupted.

Please keep me informed on the status of my case.

Yours faithfully

Name _____

Address _____

_____

Tel. _____

GENERAL ASSIGNMENT

THIS AGREEMENT IS MADE the _____ day of _____ 19 _____

BETWEEN

(1) _____ (the "Assignor"); and

(2) _____ (the "Assignee").

NOW IT IS HEREBY AGREED as follows:

1.   In consideration for the payment of £_____, receipt of which the Assignor hereby acknowledges, the Assignor hereby unconditionally and irrevocably assigns and transfers to the Assignee all right, title and interest in the following:

_____

_____

_____

2.   The Assignor fully warrants that it has full rights and authority to enter into this assignment and that the rights and benefits assigned hereunder are free and clear of any lien, encumbrance, adverse claim or interest by any third party.

3.   This assignment shall be binding upon and inure to the benefit of the parties, and their successors and assigns.

IN WITNESS OF WHICH the parties have signed this agreement the day and year first above written.

_____   _____
Signed by or on behalf of the Employee   Signed by or on behalf of the Employer

_____   _____
in the presence of (witness)   in the presence of (witness)

Name _____   Name _____

Address _____   Address _____

_____   _____
Occupation   Occupation

GENERAL COMMERCIAL SERVICES COMPLAINT

Date _____

To _____

_____

_____

Dear Sirs

On _____ I used the services of your firm for the following:_____
_____.

Under the Supply of Goods and Services Act 1982 you are under a duty to carry out your services with reasonable skill and care using materials of suitable quality, at reasonable cost and in reasonable time. However, I consider that the service you provided me was deficient for the following reason(s):_____
_____
_____.

I therefore hold you in breach of contract and am entitled to compensation for the [loss][damage] I have suffered and consider £ _____ to be a reasonable amount.

I look forward to receiving you cheque for this amount within 10 days.

Yours faithfully

_____

Name _____

Address _____

_____

Tel. _____

73

GENERAL POWER OF ATTORNEY

(Pursuant to the Powers of Attorney Act 1971, section 10)

THIS GENERAL POWER OF ATTORNEY is made

this _____ day of _____ 19 ____

BY _____

    OF _____

_____

I APPOINT _____

_____

[jointly][jointly and severally] to be my attorney(s) in accordance with section 10 of the Powers of Attorney Act 1971.

IN WITNESS whereof I have hereunto set my hand the day and year first above written.

SIGNED as a Deed and Delivered by the

    said _____

    in the presence of _____

GENERAL RELEASE

THIS DEED IS MADE the _____ day of _____ 19 _____

BETWEEN

(1) _____ (the "First Party"); and

(2) _____ (the "Second Party").

NOW IT IS HEREBY AGREED as follows:

1. The First Party forever releases, discharges, acquits and forgives the Second Party from any and all claims, actions, suits, demands, agreements, liabilities, judgment, and proceedings arising from the beginning of time to the date of these presents and as more particularly related to or arising from:

_____

_____

_____

_____

2. This release shall be binding upon and inure to the benefit of the parties, their successors and assigns.

IN WITNESS OF WHICH the parties have executed this deed the date and year first above written.

(Individual)   (Company)

                                                Signed for and on behalf of
_____
Signed by the First Party
                                                _____ Ltd
_____
in the presence of (witness)
Name _____   _____
Address _____   Director
_____   _____
Occupation _____   Director/Secretary

                                                Signed for and on behalf of
_____
Signed by the Second Party
                                                _____ Ltd
_____
in the presence of (witness)
Name _____   _____
Address _____   Director
_____   _____
Occupation _____   Director/Secretary

75

GOODS DEFECTIVE:
MANUFACTURER'S DAMAGE LIABILITY CLAIM

Date _____

To _____

_____

_____

Ref _____

Dear Sirs

I purchased the item described above from _____ (shop) of
_____ on _____.

On _____, the following serious defects became evident _____
_____
by directly causing the following [injury][damage]: _____to
_____.

As [manufacturer][own-label marketeer][first importer into the EU] of this product you are liable under the Consumer Protection Act 1987 for this injury, caused by your inherently defective goods.

I am taking legal advice on the amount of compensation I should claim based on [pain and suffering][time off work][lost wages][and property damage] and will keep you informed regarding this matter.

Yours sincerely

_____

Name _____

Address _____

_____

Tel. _____

GOODS DEFECTIVE:
RETAILER'S DAMAGE LIABILITY CLAIM

Date _____

To _____

_____

_____

Ref _____

Dear _____

I bought the above item on _____. On _____ the following serious defect became apparent _____, by causing the following damage to my property:_____, as shown in the enclosed photographs. The damage cost £_____ to repair.

Under the amended Sale of Goods Act 1979 all goods sold must be of satisfactory quality and as retailer you are liable for any damage caused by faulty goods. The very fact that the product developed a fault only ____ days after purchase means that the item was inherently faulty at the time of purchase and not of satisfactory quality, which constitutes your breach of contract.

I therefore wish to exercise my rights under the Sale of Goods Act: I am returning the goods and claim from you a full refund of the purchase price, as per the enclosed receipt plus £_____ for damage to my property.

If I do not receive a cheque within 10 days I shall have no alternative but to issue a county court summons for recovery of the amount owed to me without further notice.

Yours sincerely

_____

Name

Address

_____

GOODS DEFECTIVE:
RETAILER'S DENIAL OF LIABILITY REJECTION

Date _____

To _____

_____

_____

_____

Dear _____

Thank you for your letter of _____, in response to my complaint about _____ which I purchased from you on _____., in which you defer liability to the manufacturer.

As I stated previously, the law imposes a duty on the retailer to supply goods of satisfactory quality under the amended Sale of Goods Act 1979. On purchase of the item I entered into a contract with you, not the manufacturer; any claim I may have against the manufacturer is a separate issue. The fact that the product became faulty just _____ days after purchase proves that the item was inherently defective at the time of purchase, which constitutes your breach of contract

I therefore request that without charge you [replace the item][repair the item, while reserving my rights to full compensation should the repairs prove unsatisfactory] as I am legally entitled to do. Please note that I am not obliged to return the goods; it is your responsibility to repossess them.

I look forward to receiving your confirmation of the above within 10 days.

Yours sincerely

_____

Name _____

Address _____

_____

Tel. _____

GOODS DEFECTIVE:
FREE REPAIR REQUEST

Date _____

To _____

_____

_____

Ref _____

Dear _____

I purchased the item described above on _____. On _____ , I discovered the following serious defects: _____

_____.

Under the amended Sale of Goods Act 1979 all goods sold must be of reasonable quality. The fact that the product became faulty only _____ days after purchase proves that the item was inherently defective at the time of purchase, which constitutes your breach of contract.

I offer you the opportunity to repair the item free of charge and pay for all delivery costs, while maintaining my rights to a full refund under the Sale of Goods Act should you not repair the item or your repairs prove faulty.

Please send me a written response detailing your proposal within 10 days.

Yours sincerely

_____

Name _____

Address _____

_____

Tel. _____

GOODS NOT RECEIVED:
PROMPT DELIVERY REQUEST

Date _____

To _____

_____

_____

Ref _____

Dear _____

I have yet to receive the item described above, for which I made full payment on _____ .

You are required by the Sale of Goods Act 1979 to deliver the goods within reasonable time. Accordingly, unless I receive the goods before_____, I will consider you in breach of contract as the law entitles me to and I shall expect you to reimburse me with the full purchase price of £_____.

Please advise me as soon as possible of your intentions in this matter.

Yours sincerely

_____

Name _____

Address _____

_____

Tel. _____

GOODS UNSUITABLE: REFUND REQUEST

Date _____

To _____

_____

_____

Ref _____

Dear _____

At the suggestion of one of your sales staff, I purchased the above item on _____.

I have since discovered that it does not match the purpose or description, for which I bought it, as described by your member of staff. The reasons for my dissatisfaction are:_____

_____

_____.

Under Section 14 of the amended Sale of Goods Act 1979 all goods sold must match the purpose or description indicated by the retailer at the time of purchase. The unsuitability of this product constitutes your breach of contract, and I wish to exercise my rights under the Sale of Goods Act. I am therefore returning the _____ and claim from you a full refund of the purchase price (£_____) as per the enclosed receipt, plus delivery costs.

Please send me a cheque for this sum within 10 days. Otherwise, I shall have no alternative but to issue a county court summons for recovery of the amount owed to me without further notice.

Yours sincerely

_____

Name _____

Address _____

_____

Tel. _____

HIRE PURCHASE AGREEMENT:
DEFECTIVE PRODUCT REJECTION

Date _____

To _____

_____

_____

Ref _____

Dear _____

After following through on a hire purchase agreement with you, I received _____ _____ from the supplier on _____. On _____ I discovered the following serious defect with the product: _____

_____

_____.

Because of this problem I hereby exercise my right to reject the product under the Supply of Goods (Implied Terms) Act 1973 and to terminate our agreement.

I request that you collect the _____ and reimburse me the sum of £_____, which includes the deposit and all instalments to date, as I am legally entitled to do. A failure to pick up the _____ will result in a storage charge of £___p per day.

As of the date of this letter, I will make no further instalment payments and am not amenable to any suggestions that the faulty product be repaired. I trust you will inform me of your arrangements to pick up the goods and reimburse me in due course.

Yours sincerely

_____

Name _____

Address _____

_____

Tel. _____

HOLIDAY COMPANY COMPLAINT

Date _____

To _____

_____

_____

Ref _____

Dear _____

I am writing to express my disappointment regarding a recent holiday I took with your company on _____ to _____, costing £_____.

The [hotel][self-catering accommodation] was [substandard][not as described/shown in your _____brochure] for the following reasons:_____

_____

_____.

On _____ I complained about this to your local courier _____, but nothing was done to improve the sitauation [and no appropriate alternative accommodation was offered].

I paid for this holiday on the understanding that the accommodation would match the brochure description and photographs, which form part of the contract between ourselves. It clearly did not, judging by [the enclosed photographs][the enclosed testimonials of other holidaymakers], nor was it of a standard one would expect of a holiday of this type and price. I am therefore holding you in breach of contract and am claiming compensation for the disappointment and loss of enjoyment suffered [and for additional expenses incurred as a result of the above for which I am enclosing receipts]. In the circumstances I consider £_____ to be a reasonable compensatory sum.

I look forward to receiving your offer within 10 days. Failing that I will pursue the matter in the county court without further notice.

Yours sincerely

_____

Name _____

Address _____

_____

Tel. _____

HOLIDAY INSURANCE: CANCELLED TRIP CLAIM

Date _____

To _____

_____

_____

Ref _____

Dear _____

I arranged holiday reservations on _____ with tour operators _____ from _____ to _____ going to _____.

I have been forced to cancel my plans as a result of the following illness: _____ _____. .

Because these health-related circumstances were beyond my control, I am seeking full reimbursement, as I am entitled to do under my travel insurance policy, of _____ for all payments I have made to date. My GP, Dr _____ of _____ can, if required, provide written evidence that I was unfit for travel.

Please notify me of anything I can do to assist in processing this claim.

Yours sincerely

_____

Name _____

Address _____

_____

Tel. _____

HOLIDAY INSURANCE CLAIM

Date _____

To _____

_____

_____

Ref _____

Dear _____

I am writing to advise you that I want to claim on my holiday insurance policy no. _____.

I went on holiday to _____ from _____ to _____ and have just arrived back home. On _____ my _____, valued at £_____, was _____. I reported the matter to the local police and have written confirmation from them of this.

Please send me a claim form so I can pursue my claim.

Yours sincerely

_____

Name _____

Address _____

_____

Tel. _____

HOLIDAY LETTING AGREEMENT
(for a Holiday Let of Furnished Property)

The **PROPERTY**   _____

_____

The **LANDLORD**   _____

_____

_____

The **TENANT**   _____

_____

_____

_____

The **TERM**   _____ day(s)/week(s)/month(s)* beginning at 12 noon on _____

and expiring at 10 am on _____

(*delete as appropriate)

The **RENT**   £ _____ per week/month* payable in advance on the __ of each week/month*

or

£ _____payable in advance on the date of this Agreement

The **DEPOSIT**   £ _____

The **INVENTORY**   means the list of the Landlord's possessions at the Property which has been signed by the Landlord and the Tenant

DATED   _____

SIGNED   _____   _____

_____   _____

(The Landlord)   _____

(The Tenant)

THIS RENTAL AGREEMENT comprises the particulars detailed above and the terms and conditions printed overleaf whereby the Property is hereby let by the Landlord and taken by the Tenant for the Term at the Rent.

IMPORTANT NOTICE TO LANDLORDS:

This Form is intended for use only for a Holiday Let. If the circumstances make it clear that the letting is NOT for the purposes of the Tenant's holiday, for example because the Term is so long, the Courts may hold that it is an Assured Shorthold Tenancy (and you will not be able to obtain an order for possession of the Property for at least six months from the beginning of the tenancy).

86

Terms & Conditions on next page

HOLIDAY LETTING AGREEMENT
Terms and Conditions

1. This Agreement is a Holiday Let solely for the purpose of the Tenant's holiday in the _____ area. This tenancy is accordingly not an assured shorthold tenancy

2. The Tenant will:

2.1 pay the Rent at the times and in the manner aforesaid without any deduction abatement or set-off whatsoever

2.2 keep the interior of the Property in a good, clean and tenantable state and condition and not damage or injure the Property or any part of it

2.3 yield up the Property at the end of the Term in the same clean state and condition it was in at the beginning of the Term reasonable wear and tear and damage by insured risks excepted

2.4 maintain at the Property and keep in a good and clean condition all of the contents of the Property as listed on the Inventory, if any, and to replace or cleanse any item(s) which become broken or damaged during the Term

2.5 not make any alteration or addition to the Property nor to do any redecoration or painting of the Property

2.6 not do or omit to do anything on or at the Property which may be or become a nuisance or annoyance to the Landlord or owners or occupiers of adjoining or nearby premises or which may in any way prejudice the insurance of the Property or cause an increase in the premium payable therefor

2.7 not without the Landlord's prior consent allow or keep any pet or any kind or animal at the Property

2.8 not use or occupy the Property in any way whatsoever other than as a private holiday residence for a maximum of _____ persons

2.9 not assign, sublet, charge or part with or share possession of occupation of the Property or any part thereof

2.10 permit the Landlord or anyone authorised by the Landlord at reasonable hours in the daytime and upon reasonable prior notice (except in emergency) to enter and view the Property for any proper purpose (including the checking of compliance with the Tenant's obligations under this Agreement and during the last month of the Term the showing of the Property to prospective new tenants)

2.11 pay interest at the rate of 4% above the Base Lending Rate for the time being of the Landlord's bankers upon any Rent or other money due from the Tenant under this Agreement which is more than 3 days in arrear in respect of the period from when it became due to the date of payment

2.12 pay for all telephone calls and services made at or rendered to the Property (except for the standing charge) during the Term

3. Subject to the Tenant paying the rent and performing his/her obligations under this Agreement the Tenant may peaceably hold and enjoy the Property during the term without interruption from the Landlord or any person rightfully claiming under or in trust for the Landlord

4. The Landlord will insure the Property and the contents of the Property which belong the Landlord, as listed on the Inventory, if any

5. In the event of the Rent being unpaid for more than 10 days after it is due (whether demanded or not) or there being a breach of any other of the Tenant's obligations under this Agreement then the Landlord may re-enter the Property and this Rental Agreement shall thereupon determine absolutely but without prejudice to any of the Landlord's other rights and remedies in respect of any outstanding obligations on the part of the Tenant

6. The Deposit has been paid by the Tenant and is held by the Landlord to secure compliance with the Tenant's obligations under this Agreement (without prejudice to the Landlord's other rights and remedies) and if, at any time during the Term, the Landlord is obliged to draw upon it to satisfy any outstanding breaches of such obligations then the Tenant shall forthwith make such additional payment as is necessary to restore the full amount of the Deposit held by the Landlord. As soon as reasonably practicable following termination of this Agreement the Landlord shall return to the Tenant the Deposit or the balance thereof after any deductions properly made

7. The Landlord hereby notifies the Tenant under Section 48 of the Landlord & Tenant Act 1987 that any notices (including notices in proceedings) should be served upon the Landlord at the address stated with the name of the Landlord overleaf

8. In the event of damage to or destruction of the Property by any of the risks insured against by the Landlord the Tenant shall be relieved from payment of the Rent to the extent that the Tenant's use and enjoyment of the Property is thereby prevented and from performance of its obligations as to the state and condition of the Property to the extent of and so long as there prevails such damage or destruction (except to the extent that the insurance is prejudiced by any act or default of the Tenant)

9. Where the context so admits:

9.1 The "Landlord" includes the persons for the time being entitled to the reversion expectant upon this Tenancy

9.2 The "Tenant" includes any persons deriving title under the Tenant

9.3 The "Property" includes all of the Landlord's fixtures and fittings at or upon the Property

9.4 The "Term" shall mean the period stated in the particulars overleaf or any shorter or longer period in the event of an earlier termination or an extension respectively

10. All references to the singular shall include the plural and vice versa and any obligations or liabilities of more than one person shall be joint and several and an obligation on the part of a party shall include an obligation not to allow or permit the breach of that obligation

HOUSE RULES
(for Lodgers/B&B Guests)

1. The price for the use of the room (with bed and breakfast and evening meal*) is £_____ per week payable in advance on _____ of each week.

2. The room will be cleaned and sheets changed on _____ of each week.

3. Guests are requested to keep the room tidy and not to bring any food into it.

4. No overnight visitors are permitted. Any visitors must leave the premises at 10 p.m. when the doors will be locked.

5. The volume control on any television, radio, audio system or musical instrument must be turned low so that they are not audible from outside the room. The owner reserves the right to require these to be turned off if they cause annoyance to them or other occupiers.

6. Communal bathroom and kitchen facilities (if any) must be left clean and tidy by guests after use.

7. Guests may use the sitting room.

8. Guests have use of the bedroom assigned to them but they do not have exclusive possession of it. The owner reserves the right to require the guest to move to another room at short notice.

9. Guests must not move furniture, pictures or wall hangings without the consent of the owner, nor should they install their own furniture, pictures or wall hanging without such consent.

10. Guests returning to the house after 10 p.m. without prior arrangement with the owner are liable to be locked out.

* Delete as appropriate

HOUSE/FLAT SHARE AGREEMENT
(a Licence for Shared Occupation of a Furnished House or Flat – Non-Resident Owner)

The PROPERTY _____

_____

The Owner _____

of _____

The Sharer _____

_____

The PERIOD _____ weeks/months* beginning on _____

EARLY TERMINATION
(delete if not required)

⌈ Either party may at any time end this Licence earlier than the end of the Period ⌉ (* delete as appropriate)
⌊ by giving to the other written notice of _____ week(s)/month(s)* ⌋

The PAYMENT £ _____ per week/month* payable in advance on the _____ of each week/month*

The Deposit £ _____

The Inventory means the list of the Owner's possessions at the Property which has been signed by the Owner and the Sharer

DATED _____

SIGNED _____   _____

_____   _____

(The Owner)   (The Sharer)

THIS HOUSE/FLAT SHARE LICENCE comprises the particulars detailed above and the terms and conditions printed overleaf whereby the Property is licensed by the Owner and taken by the Sharer for occupation with up to _____ other sharers during the Period upon making the Payment.

IMPORTANT NOTICE:

(1) **This form of Licence does not require either party to give any form of notice to the other at the end of the fixed Period but if either party wishes to end this Licence early as referred to in the definition of 'the PERIOD' near the middle of this Licence then the Notice to Terminate may be used.**

*(2) **The law requires that the written notice should not be less than four weeks in the case of notices given by Non-Resident Owners (for whom this Licence is intended).**

Terms and Conditions on next page

HOUSE/FLAT SHARE AGREEMENT
Non-Resident Owner
Terms and Conditions

1. The Sharer will:

1.1 be allowed to share with the other occupiers of the Property the use and facilities of the Property (including such bathroom, toilet, kitchen and sitting room facilities as may be at the Property)

1.2 pay the Payment at the times and in the manner aforesaid without any deduction or abatement or set-off whatsoever

1.3 make a proportionate contribution to the cost of all charges in respect of any electric, gas, water and telephonic or televisual services used at or supplied to the Property and Council Tax or any similar tax that might be charged in addition to or replacement of it during the Period

1.4 keep the interior of the Property in a good clean and tenantable state and condition and not damage or injure the Property or any part of it and if at the end of the Period any item on the Inventory requires repair, replacing, cleaning or laundering the Sharer will pay for the same (reasonable wear and tear and damage by an insured risk excepted)

1.5 maintain at the Property and keep in a good and clean condition all of the items listed in the Inventory

1.6 not make any alteration or addition to the Property nor without the Owner's prior written consent to do any redecoration or painting of the Property

1.7 not do or omit to do anything on or at the Property which may be or become a nuisance or annoyance to the Owner or any other occupiers of the Property or owners or occupiers of adjoining or nearby premises or which may in any way prejudice the insurance of the Property or cause an increase in the premium payable therefor

1.8 not without the Owner's prior consent allow or keep any pet or any kind of animal at the property

1.9 not use or occupy the Property in any way whatsoever other than as a private residence

1.10 cook at the Property only in the kitchen

1.11 not part with or share possession or occupation of the Property or any part thereof

1.12 pay interest at the rate of 4% above the Base Lending Rate for the time being of the Owner's bankers upon any payment or other money due from the Sharer under this Licence which is more than 3 days in arrear in respect of the period from when it become due down to the date of payment

2. In the event of the Payment being unpaid for more than 10 days after it is due (whether demanded or not) or there being a breach of any other of the Sharer's obligations under this Licence or in the event of the Sharer ceasing to reside at the Property or in the event of the Sharer's death this Licence shall thereupon determine absolutely but without prejudice to any of the Owner's other rights and remedies in respect of any outstanding obligations on the part of the Sharer

3. The Deposit has been paid by the Sharer and is held by the Owner to secure compliance with the Sharer's obligations under this Licence (without prejudice to the Owner's other rights and remedies) and if, at any time during the Period, the Owner is obliged to draw upon it to satisfy any outstanding breaches of such obligations then the Sharer shall forthwith make such additional payment as is necessary to restore the full amount of the Deposit held by the Owner. As soon as reasonably practicable following determination of this Licence the Owner shall return to the Sharer the Deposit or the balance thereof after any deductions properly made

4. The Owner will insure the Property and the items listed on the Inventory

5. The Owner hereby notifies the Sharer that any notices (including notices in proceedings) should be served upon the Owner at the address stated with the name of the Owner overleaf

6. In the event of damage to or destruction of the Property by any of the risks insured against by the Owner the Sharer shall be relieved from making the Payment to the extent that the Sharer's use and enjoyment of the Property is thereby prevented and from performance of its obligations as to the state and condition of the Property to the extent of and whilst there prevails any such damage or destruction (except to the extent that the insurance is prejudiced by any act or default of the Sharer) the amount in case of dispute to be settled by arbitration

7. As long as the reference to a notice of early termination in the definition of the "PERIOD" overleaf (the "early termination notice") has not been deleted then either party may at any time during the Period terminate this Licence by giving to the other prior written notice to that effect, the length of such notice to be that stated in the early termination notice, and upon the expiry of said notice this Licence shall end with no further liability for either party save for liability for any antecedent breach

8. The Sharer shall not have exclusive possession of any part of the Property and the identity of the other occupiers of the Property shall be in the absolute discretion of the Owner

9. Where the context so admits:

9.1 the "Property" includes all of the Owner's fixtures and fittings at or upon the Property and all of the items listed in the Inventory and (for the avoidance of doubt) the Room

9.2 the "Period" shall mean the period stated in the particulars overleaf or any shorter or longer period in the event of an earlier termination or an extension of the Licence respectively

10. All references to the singular shall include the plural and vice versa and any obligations or liabilities of more than one person shall be joint and several and an obligation on the part of a party shall include an obligation not to allow or permit the breach of that obligation

HOUSE/FLAT SHARE AGREEMENT
(for a Room in a Furnished House or Flat – Resident Owner)

The PROPERTY _____

_____

The ROOM   means the room at the Property which has been nominated by the Owner and agreed to by the Sharer

The OWNER _____

_____ whose address is the Property above

The SHARER _____

_____

The PERIOD _____ weeks/months* beginning on _____

EARLY TERMINATION
(delete if not required)

⎡ Either party may at any time end this Agreement earlier than the end of the Period ⎤ (* delete as appropriate)
⎣ by giving to the other written notice of _____ week(s)/month(s)* ⎦

The PAYMENT   £ _____ per week/month* payable in advance on the _____ of each week/month*

The DEPOSIT   £_____

The INVENTORY   means the list of the Owner's possessions at the Property which has been signed by the Owner and the Sharer

DATED _____

SIGNED _____   _____

           _____   _____

              (The Owner)   (The Sharer)

THIS HOUSE/FLAT SHARE AGREEMENT comprises the particulars detailed above and the terms and conditions printed overleaf whereby the Property is licensed by the Owner and taken by the Sharer for occupation during the Period upon making the Payment.

IMPORTANT NOTICE:

(1)   This form of Agreement is for use in those cases where the Room is part of a House or Flat which the Owner occupies as his/her only or principal home so that an assured tenancy is not created.

(2)   This form of Agreement does not require either party to give any form of notice to the other at the end of the fixed Period but if either party wishes to end this Agreement early as referred to in the definition of the PERIOD near the middle of this Agreement then the Notice to Terminate may be used.

Terms and Conditions on next page

HOUSE/FLAT SHARE AGREEMENT
Resident Owner

Terms and Conditions

1. The Sharer will:

1.1 in conjunction with the occupation of the Room only be allowed to share with the other occupiers of the Property the use and facilities of the common parts of the Property (including such bathroom, toilet, kitchen and sitting room facilities as may be at the Property)

1.2 pay the Payment at the times and in the manner aforesaid without any deduction or abatement or set-off whatsoever

1.3 make a proportionate contribution to the cost of all charges in respect of any electric, gas, water and telephonic or televisual services used at or supplied to the Property and Council Tax or any similar tax that might be charged in addition to or replacement of it during the Period

1.4 keep the Room and share with the other occupiers of the Property the obligation to keep the interior of the Property in a good clean and tenantable state and condition and not damage or injure the Property or any part of it and if at the end of the Period any item on the Inventory requires repair replacing cleaning or laundering the Sharer will pay for the same (reasonable wear and tear and damage by an insured risk excepted)

1.5 yield up the Room at the end of the Period in the same clean state and condition it was in at the beginning of the Period

1.6 share with the other occupiers of the Property the obligation to maintain at the Property and keep in a good and clean condition all of the items listed in the Inventory

1.7 not make any alteration or addition to the Property nor without the Owner's prior written consent to do any redecoration or painting of the Property

1.8 not do or omit to do anything on or at the Property which may be or become a nuisance or annoyance to the Owner or any other occupiers of the Property or owners or occupiers of adjoining or nearby premises or which may in any way prejudice the insurance of the Property or cause an increase in the premium payable therefor

1.9 not without the Owner's prior consent allow or keep any pet or any kind of animal at the Property

1.10 not use or occupy the Property in any way whatsoever other than as a private residence

1.11 not assign, sublet, charge or part with or share possession or occupation of the Room or the Property or any part thereof

1.12 pay interest at the rate of 4% above the Base Lending Rate for the time being of the Owner's bankers upon any payment or other money due from the Sharer under this Agreement which is more than 3 days in arrear in respect of the period from when it become due down to the date of payment

2. In the event of the Payment being unpaid for more than 10 days after it is due (whether demanded or not) or there being a breach of any other of the Sharer's obligations under this Agreement then the Owner may re-enter the Room and this Agreement shall thereupon determine absolutely but without prejudice to any of the Owner's other rights and remedies in respect of any outstanding obligations on the part of the Sharer

3. The Deposit has been paid by the Sharer and is held by the Owner to secure compliance with the Sharer's obligations under this Agreement (without prejudice to the Owner's other rights and remedies) and if, at any time during the Period, the Owner is obliged to draw upon it to satisfy any outstanding breaches of such obligations then the Sharer shall forthwith make such additional payment as is necessary to restore the full amount of the Deposit held by the Owner. As soon as reasonably practicable following determination of this Agreement the Owner shall return to the Sharer the Deposit or the balance thereof after any deductions properly made

4. The Owner will insure the Property and the items listed on the Inventory

5. The Owner hereby notifies the Sharer that any notices (including notices in proceedings) should be served upon the Owner at the address stated with the name of the Owner overleaf

6. In the event of damage to or destruction of the Property by any of the risks insured against by the Owner the Sharer shall be relieved from making the Payment to the extent that the Sharer's use and enjoyment of the Property is thereby prevented and from performance of its obligations as to the state and condition of the Property to the extent of and whilst there prevails any such damage or destruction (except to the extent that the insurance is prejudiced by any act or default of the Sharer) the amount in case of dispute to be settled by arbitration

7. As long as the reference to a notice of early termination in the definition of the "PERIOD" overleaf (the "early termination notice") has not been deleted then either party may at any time during the Period terminate this Agreement by giving to the other prior written notice to that effect, the length of such notice to be that stated in the early termination notice, and upon the expiry of said notice this Agreement shall end with no further liability for either party save for liability for any antecedent breach

8. The Owner may at any time nominate for the Sharer another room in the Property in replacement of the Room occupied by the Sharer until that point ("the replacement Room") and all reference in this Agreement to the "Room" shall thenceforth be deemed to refer to the replacement Room and this process may be repeated by the Owner any number of times during the Period PROVIDED THAT the Sharer may after such a nomination give to the Owner an early termination notice as referred to in clause 6 above and be allowed to remain in the Room occupied prior to the said nomination until the expiry of the said early termination notice

9. The Sharer shall not have exclusive possession of the Room and the identity of the other occupiers of the Property shall be in the absolute discretion of the Owner

10. Where the context so admits:

10.1 the "Property" includes all of the Owner's fixtures and fittings at or upon the Property and all of the items listed in the Inventory and (for the avoidance of doubt) the Room

10.2 the "Period" shall mean the period stated in the particulars overleaf or any shorter or longer period in the event of an earlier termination or an extension or holding over respectively

11. All references to the singular shall include the plural and vice versa and any obligations or liabilities of more than one person shall be joint and several and an obligation on the part of a party shall include an obligation not to allow or permit the breach of that obligation

HOUSEHOLD INVENTORY

Re _____ (the Property)

No.	Living Room	No.		No.	
____	Armchair	____	Casserole dish	____	Pyrex dish
____	Ashtray	____	Cheese grater	____	Roasting dish
____	Chairs	____	Chopping board	____	Rolling pin
____	Coffee table	____	Coffee pot	____	Salt & pepper pots
____	Curtains	____	Corkscrew	____	Sauce pans
____	Cushions	____	Cups	____	Scales
____	Framed picture	____	Dessert spoons	____	Serving dishes
____	Stereo system	____	Dinner plates	____	Side plates
____	Mirror	____	Dishwasher	____	Sieve
____	Net curtains	____	Draining board	____	Soup spoons
____	Plant	____	Egg cups	____	Spatula
____	Rug	____	Forks	____	Storage jars
____	Sofa	____	Fridge/Freezer	____	Sugar jug
____	Table	____	Fruit bowl	____	Swing bin
____	Table lamp	____	Frying pans	____	Table
____	Tel.	____	Garlic crusher	____	Tablecloth
____	Television	____	Glasses	____	Table mats
____	Vase	____	Kettle	____	Teapot
____	Video	____	Knives	____	Tea spoons
____	Wall clock	____	Liquidiser	____	Tea towels
____		____	Measuring jug	____	Tin opener
____		____	Microwave	____	Toaster
		____	Milk jug	____	Tray
No.	**Kitchen/Dining Room**	____	Mugs	____	Washing machine
____	Apron	____	Mug tree	____	Washing up bowl
____	Baking tray	____	Oven & Hob	____	Wok
____	Bottle opener	____	Pie dishes	____	Wooden spoons
____	Bread bin	____	Potato peeler	____	
____	Carving knives	____	Pudding/Soup dishes	____	

No.	Bedroom One	No.		No.	
____	Blankets	____	Chair	____	Soap dish
____	Bed sheets	____	Chest of drawers	____	Towels
____	Chair	____	Curtains	____	Wall mirror
____	Chest of drawers	____	Double bed	____	Wooden chair
____	Curtains	____	Dressing table	____	
____	Double bed	____	Duvet	____	
____	Dressing table	____	Duvet cover		
____	Duvet	____	Framed picture	**No.**	**Storage cupboard**
____	Duvet cover	____	Lamp	____	Broom
____	Framed picture	____	Mattress cover	____	Bucket
____	Lamp	____	Net curtains	____	Clothes horse
____	Mattress cover	____	Pillows	____	Dustpan & brush
____	Net curtains	____	Pillow cases	____	Iron
____	Pillows	____	Side table	____	Ironing board
____	Pillow cases	____	Single bed	____	Mop
____	Side table	____	Table mirror	____	Vacuum cleaner
____	Single bed	____	Wall mirror	____	
____	Table mirror	____	Wardrobe	____	
____	Wall mirror	____			
____	Wardrobe	____		**No.**	**Hall**
____				____	Coat stand
____		**No.**	**Bathroom**	____	Framed picture
		____	Basket	____	
No.	**Bedroom Two**	____	Floor mat	____	
____	Blankets	____	Lavatory brush		
____	Bed sheets	____	Shower curtain		

Signed _____   _____

      (Landlord/Owner)   (Tenant/Sharer)

IMPORTANT DOCUMENT LOCATOR

OF

Name _____

Will _____

Birth
Certificate _____

Marriage
Certificate _____

Divorce Decree _____

Title Deeds _____

Mortgage
Documents _____

Life Insurance
Policies _____

Pension Details _____

Share
Certificates _____

Other Investment
Certificates _____

Loan and H.P.
Agreements _____

Bank Account
Details _____

Building Society
Passbooks _____

Donor Cards _____

Passport _____

INDEMNITY AGREEMENT

THIS DEED IS MADE the _____ day of _____ 19 _____

BETWEEN

(1) _____ (the "First Party"); and

(2) _____ (the "Second Party").

NOW THIS DEED WITNESSES as follows:

1.   The First Party agrees to indemnify and save harmless the Second Party and its successors and assigns, from any claim, action, liability, loss, damage or suit, arising from the following:

_____

_____

2.   In the event of any asserted claim, the Second Party shall provide the First Party immediate written notice of the same, and thereafter the First Party shall at its own expense defend, protect and save harmless the Second Party against that claim or any loss or liability thereunder.

3.   In the event the First Party shall fail to so defend and/or indemnify and save harmless, then in such instance the Second Party shall have the right to defend, pay or settle the claim on its own behalf without notice to the First Party and with full rights of recourse against the the First Party for all fees, costs, expenses and payments made or agreed to be paid to discharge the claim.

4.   Upon default, the First Party further agrees to pay all reasonable solicitor's fees necessary to enforce this Agreement.

5.   This Agreement shall be unlimited as to amount or duration.

6.   This Agreement shall be binding upon and inure to the benefit of the parties, their successors and assigns.

IN WITNESS OF WHICH the parties have executed this Deed the day and year first above written.

(Individual)   (Company)

_____   Signed for and on behalf of
Signed by the First Party
                                                                            Ltd
_____   _____
in the presence of (witness)
Name _____   _____
Address _____   Director
_____
Occupation _____   Director/Secretary

_____   Signed for and on behalf of:
Signed by the Second Party
                                                                            Ltd
_____   _____
in the presence of (witness)
Name _____
Address _____   _____
_____   Director

Occupation _____   _____
                                                       Director/Secretary

INSURANCE CLAIM NOTICE

Date _____

To _____

_____

_____

Ref _____

Dear _____

You are hereby notified that I have incurred a loss which I believe is covered by my insurance policy detailed below. Details of the loss are as follows:

1. Type of loss or claim: _____

2. Date and time incurred:_____

3. Location: _____

4. Estimated loss: _____

I am able to provide documentary evidence to support my claim as necessary. Please forward a claim form to me as soon as possible.

Yours sincerely

_____

Name _____

Address _____

_____

Tel. No. (Work) _____

Tel. No. (Home) _____

Policy Number _____

INSURANCE CLAIM DISPUTE: REFERRAL TO OMBUDSMAN

Date _____

To The Insurance Ombudsman Bureau
135 Park Street
London SE1 9EA

Ref _____

Dear Sirs

I have been in dispute with the above named insurance company for _____ weeks over the following issue: _____. I have used the company's complaints procedure exhaustively, but the complaint has yet to be resolved.

I believe the firm is a member of your scheme and I am therefore referring the matter to you for investigation. Please review the enclosed correspondence regarding my case.

I look forward to hearing from you in due course.

Yours faithfully

_____

Name _____

Address _____

_____

Tel. _____

INSURANCE CLAIM FOR PROPERTY DAMAGE

Date _____

To _____

_____

_____

Ref _____

Dear _____

I am writing to confirm that I want make a claim for damage to my property located at _____ under policy no._____.

The following damage was inflicted on the property on _____ at _____as a direct result of _____
_____.

The interim repair bill came to £_____ ; additional work costing £_____ is required to complete damage repairs.

I am enclosing documentary [and photographic] evidence of the cause of the damage and a written report on the temporary damage repairs from the above firm and an estimate of the work needed to complete repairs.

Please send me the appropriate form so I may complete my claim.

Yours sincerely

_____

_____

Name _____

Address _____

_____

Tel. _____

INSURANCE POLICY ASSIGNMENT

THIS DEED is made the _____ day of _____ 19_____

BETWEEN:

(1) _____ of _____ (the "Assignor"); and

(2) _____ of _____ (the "Assignee").

WHEREAS:

(A) The Assignor is the holder of a Policy of Insurance number _____ issued by the _____ Insurance Company (the "Policy").

(B) The Assignor wishes to assign the benefit of the Policy to the Assignee.

NOW THIS DEED WITNESSES as follows:

1.   The Assignor warrants that the Policy is in full force and effect and all premiums thereon have been paid in full to date.

2.   The Assignor further warrants that he/she has full authority to transfer the Policy, and shall execute all further documents as may be required by the Insurance Company or broker to effect this Assignment.

3.   The Assignor hereby assigns to the Assignee and the Assignee hereby accepts the assignment of the Policy and all the obligations and benefits attaching thereto.

4.   This assignment shall by binding upon and inure to the benefit of the parties, their successors and assigns.

IN WITNESS OF WHICH the parties have executed this deed the day and year first above written.

(Individual)

_____
Signed by the Assignor

_____
in the presence of (witness)
Name
_____
Address
_____

_____
Occupation

_____
Signed by the Assignee

_____
in the presence of (witness)
Name
_____
Address
_____

_____
Occupation

(Company)

Signed for and on behalf of

_____ Ltd

_____
Director

_____
Director/Secretary

Signed for and on behalf of:

_____ Ltd

_____
Director

_____
Director/Secretary

INVESTMENT ADVICE COMPLAINT

Date _____

To The Compliance Officer

_____

_____

Dear Sir

COMPLAINT

Ref policy number_____ Ref no._____

I am writing to complain about the above _____ investment product which I bought on _____, advised and arranged by _____.

My reasons for complaints are as follows:

_____

_____.

The Financial Services Act 1986 requires you to offer consumers best advice, taking into consideration their personal circumstances. You have clearly failed to do so judging by the performance the above product and my requirements.

Please let me know if you are unable to investigate this complaint within two months, as I may then take my complaint directly to the Personal Investment Authority Ombudsman.

I look forward to receiving your acknowledgment of this letter within seven working days.

Yours sincerely

_____

Name _____

Address _____

_____

Tel. _____

INVESTMENT ADVICE COMPLAINT:
REFERRAL TO PIA OMBUDSMAN

Date _____

To The PIA Ombudsman

Hertsmere House

Hertsmere Road

London E14 4AB

Dear Sir

Re _____

I made a written complaint to the Complaints Officer of the above firm about poor investment advice they gave me and [I am not happy with the outcome of their investigation into my case][I have not received the result of their investigation within two months of my complaint].

I should be grateful if you could send me the relevant forms for taking my complaint to you for consideration. I understand your services are free of charge.

I look forward to hearing from you.

Yours faithfully

_____

Name _____

Address _____

_____

Tel. _____

LAND PURCHASE OPTION ASSIGNMENT

THIS AGREEMENT is made the _____ day of _____ 19_____

BETWEEN:

(1) _____ of _____ (the "Assignor"); and

(2) _____ of _____ (the "Assignee").

WHEREAS:

(A) The Assignor is the holder of an option to purchase property located at _____ _____ which expires on _____ 19_____ (the "Option"), a copy of which is annexed.

(B) The Assignor wishes to sell the Option to the Assignee.

NOW IT IS HEREBY AGREED as follows:

1. In consideration for the payment of £ _____, receipt of which the Assignee hereby acknowledges, the Assignor hereby transfers his/her entire interest in the Option and all his/her rights thereunder to the Assignee.

2. The Assignor warrants that the Option is fully assignable.

3. The Assignee, by accepting the transfer of the Option, agrees to exercise the Option, if at all, according to its terms.

4. This agreement shall be binding upon and inure to the benefit of the parties, their successors and assigns.

IN WITNESS OF WHICH the parties have signed this agreement the day and year first above written.

_____   _____
Signed by or on behalf of the Assignor   Signed by or on behalf of the Assignee

_____   _____
in the presence of (witness)   in the presence of (witness)

Name _____   Name _____

Address _____   Address _____

_____   _____
Occupation   Occupation

103

LAND REGISTRY: LEASEHOLDER'S LANDLORD ENQUIRY

Date _____

To The Land Registry

Rosebrae Court

Woodside Ferry Approach

Birkenhead L41 6DU

Dear Sirs

I am writing under the authority of section 112C Land Registration Act 1925 to ask for a search to be made of my immediate landlord of the following leasehold property of which I am the leaseholder:

_____

_____

_____

Lease registration details:_____.

I look forward to hearing from you shortly.

Yours faithfully

_____

Name _____

Address _____

_____

Tel. _____

LANDLORD'S LETTER RE BILLS

Date _____

Ref _____

To _____ (name and address
                                 of Authority)

_____

_____

Dear Sir(s)

Re. _____ (the Property)

I am /we are the landlord(s) of the above property and write to advise you that with effect

from

_____ (date of start of tenancy)

the property has been let to

_____ (name(s) of Tenant(s))

_____

who will therefore be responsible with effect from that date for the [council tax] [electricity

charges] [gas charges] [telephone charges] [water rates] in respect of the property.

Yours faithfully

_____ (Landlord's signature &
                                             printed name & address)

_____

_____

_____

LANDLORD'S NOTICE CONFIRMING AGENT'S AUTHORITY

Date _____

Ref _____

To _____ (name of Tenant(s))

_____

_____

Dear Tenant(s)

Re._____ (the Property)

Please note that _____ (name & address
of agent(s))

_____

_____

is/are now authorised to deal with the above property on my/our behalf so that you should until further notice pay the rent and any other payments due under the tenancy to him/her and deal with him/her/them in respect of any other matters relating to the property.

Yours faithfully

_____ (Landlord's signature &
printed name & address)

_____

_____

106

LANDLORD'S REFERENCE REQUIREMENTS

Work reference – stating	(a) Job Title	Yes ☐	No ☐
	(b) Length of Employment	Yes ☐	No ☐
	(c) Salary	Yes ☐	No ☐
Last three payslips		Yes ☐	No ☐
If self-employed	(a) Copy of last set of accounts	Yes ☐	No ☐
	(b) accountant's letter – stating		
	(i) length of time known to accountant	Yes ☐	No ☐
	(ii) indication of yearly income	Yes ☐	No ☐

BANK/BUILDING SOCIETY

Last three bank statements	Yes ☐	No ☐
Building society book	Yes ☐	No ☐

OTHER

Student identification (e.g. student card or letter of acceptance)	Yes ☐	No ☐
Personal reference (e.g. professional friend)	Yes ☐	No ☐

Last Will & Testament
RESIDUE DIRECT TO CHILDREN

PRINT NAME AND ADDRESS

THIS Last Will and Testament is made by me _____

of _____

I REVOKE all previous wills and codicils.

EXECUTORS' NAMES AND ADDRESSES

I APPOINT as executors and trustees of my will

_____ and _____

of _____ of _____

SUBSTITUTIONAL EXECUTOR'S NAME AND ADDRESS

and should one or more of them fail to or be unable to act I APPOINT to fill any vacancy

_____

of _____

GUARDIAN'S NAME AND ADDRESS

I APPOINT _____

of _____

to be guardian of any of my children who are minors if my husband/wife dies before me.

SPECIFIC GIFTS AND LEGACIES

I GIVE _____

_____

_____

_____

_____

_____

_____

RESIDUARY GIFT

(insert age at which you want your children to inherit capital)

I GIVE the rest of my estate to my executor and trustees to hold on trust, either to sell it or (if they think fit without being liable for any loss) to retain all or any part of it and pay my debts, taxes and testamentary expenses and pay the residue to those of my children who survive me and attain the age of _____ years if more than one in equal shares.
PROVIDED THAT if any of my children dies before me or after me but under that age, I GIVE the share that child would have taken to his or her own children who attain 18 equally. If no person shall inherit the residue of my estate under the preceding gifts, I GIVE it to

_____

TRUSTEES' POWERS

IN ADDITION to their powers under the general law, my trustees may invest the balance of my estate in any manner in which they could invest their own funds. While a child is a minor, my trustees may at their absolute discretion use all or any part of the income from the child's share for the child's maintenance, education or benefit.

FUNERAL WISHES

I WISH my body to be ☐ buried ☐ cremated other instructions _____

_____

DATE

SIGNED by the above-named testator in our presence on the _____ day of _____ 19 ____
and then by us in the testator's presence

TESTATOR'S SIGNATURE

SIGNED _____

WITNESSES' SIGNATURES NAMES AND ADDRESSES

SIGNED _____ SIGNED _____

_____ _____

of _____ of _____

_____ _____

occupation _____ occupation _____

ℒast 𝔚ill & 𝔗estament

RESIDUE TO ADULT

PRINT NAME AND ADDRESS

THIS Last Will and Testament is made by me _____

of _____

EXECUTORS' NAMES AND ADDRESSES

I REVOKE all previous wills and codicils.

I APPOINT as executors and trustees of my will

_____ and _____

of _____ of _____

_____ _____

SUBSTITUTIONAL EXECUTOR'S NAME AND ADDRESS

and should one or more of them fail to or be unable to act I APPOINT to fill any vacancy

_____

of _____

SPECIFIC GIFTS AND LEGACIES

I GIVE _____

_____

_____

_____

_____

_____

_____

_____

_____

_____

_____

_____

_____

RESIDUARY GIFT

I GIVE the residue of my estate to _____

_____

but if he/she or (if I have indicated more than one person) any of them fails to survive me by 28 days or if this gift or any part of it fails for any other reason, then I GIVE the residue of my estate or the part of it affected to

_____

FUNERAL WISHES

I WISH my body to be ☐ buried ☐ cremated other instructions _____

_____

DATE

SIGNED by the above-named testator in our presence on the _____ day of _____ 19 ____
and then by us in the testator's presence

TESTATOR'S SIGNATURE

SIGNED _____

WITNESSES' SIGNATURES NAMES AND ADDRESSES

SIGNED _____ SIGNED _____

_____ _____

of _____ of _____

_____ _____

occupation _____ occupation _____

ℒast 𝔚ill & 𝔗estament
RESIDUE TO AN ADULT BUT IF HE/SHE DIES TO CHILDREN

PRINT NAME AND ADDRESS

THIS Last Will and Testament is made by me _____

of _____

I REVOKE all previous wills and codicils.

EXECUTORS' NAMES AND ADDRESSES

I APPOINT as executors and trustees of my will

_____ and _____

of _____ of _____

_____ _____

SUBSTITUTIONAL EXECUTOR'S NAME AND ADDRESS

and should one or more of them fail to or be unable to act I APPOINT to fill any vacancy

_____

of _____

GUARDIAN'S NAME AND ADDRESS

I APPOINT _____

of _____

to be guardian of any of my children who are minors if my husband/wife dies before me.

SPECIFIC GIFTS AND LEGACIES

I GIVE _____

_____

_____

_____

_____

_____

_____

RESIDUARY GIFT

I GIVE the rest of my estate to my executors and trustees to hold on trust, either to sell it or (if they think fit and without being liable for any loss) to retain all or any part of it and pay my debts, taxes and testamentary expenses and pay the residue to

_____

(insert age at which you want your children to inherit capital)

but if he/she or (if I have indicated more than one person) any of them fails to survive me by 28 days or if this gift or any part of it fails for any other reason, then I GIVE the residue of my estate or the part of it affected to those of my children who survive me and attain the age of _____ years if more then one in equal shares.
PROVIDED THAT if any of my children dies before me or after me but under that age, I GIVE the share that child would have taken to his or her own children who attain 18 equally. If no person shall inherit the residue of my estate or part of it under the preceding gifts, I GIVE it to

_____

TRUSTEES' POWERS

IN ADDITION to their powers under the general law, my trustees may invest the balance of my estate in any manner in which they could invest their own funds. While a child is a minor, my trustees may at their absolute discretion use all or any part of the income from the child's share for the child's maintenance, education or benefit.

FUNERAL WISHES

I WISH my body to be ☐ buried ☐ cremated other instructions _____

_____

DATE

SIGNED by the above-named testator in our presence on the _____ day of _____ 19 _____
and then by us in the testator's presence

TESTATOR'S SIGNATURE

SIGNED _____

WITNESSES' SIGNATURES NAMES AND ADDRESSES

SIGNED _____ SIGNED _____

_____ _____

of _____ of _____

_____ _____

occupation _____ occupation _____

LEASEHOLDER'S SERVICE CHARGE:
REQUEST FOR DOCUMENTS SUPPORTING SUMMARY

Date _____

To _____

_____

_____

Dear _____

Thank you for providing me with a summary of the accounts relating to the service charge of the below property from _____ to _____.

I am now exercising my right under s22 Landlord & Tenant Act 1987 and wish to inspect the documents supporting the summary, i.e. bills, receipts, etc. and to take copies of them. Please afford me reasonable facilities for this inspection, as you are legally bound to do. I look forward to hearing from you within seven working days.

Yours sincerely

_____

Name _____

Address _____

_____

Tel. _____

LEASEHOLDER'S SERVICE CHARGE:
REQUEST FOR SUMMARY OF LANDLORD'S ACCOUNTS

Date _____

To _____

_____

_____

Dear _____

I am writing under the authority of section 21, Landlord & Tenant Act 1987 to ask you for a summary of the accounts relating to the service charges for below property for the period _____, as I am legally entitled to do.

I look forward to hearing from you within seven working days. Please note that should you refuse to supply me with this summary I can apply to the Leasehold Valuation Tribunal for the appointment of a new Manager of the property.

Yours sincerely

_____

Name _____

Address _____

_____

Tel. _____

LETTER TO EXECUTOR

Date _____

To _____

_____

_____

Ref _____

Dear _____

I am writing to confirm that I have named you as an executor of my Will dated _____ 19 _____ .

- A copy of my Will is enclosed.*

- My signed original Will has been lodged with _____ .

- I have named _____ as a co-executor.

- My solicitor is _____ at _____ .*

Please confirm to me in writing that you are willing to act as one of my executors.

Yours sincerely

_____

Name _____

Address _____

_____

Tel. _____

* delete as necessary

WARNING: DO NOT INCLUDE ANY OTHER INSTRUCTIONS TO YOUR EXECUTORS IN THIS LETTER

LIMITED GUARANTEE

THIS AGREEMENT IS MADE the _____ day of _____ 19 _____

BETWEEN:

(1) _____ (the "Guarantor"); and

(2) _____ (the "Creditor").

NOW IT IS HEREBY AGREED as follows:

1. As an inducement to the Creditor to extend credit from time to time to _____ _____ (the "Customer") the Guarantor unconditionally guarantees to the Creditor the prompt and punctual payment of certain sums now or hereinafter due to the Creditor from the Customer, provided that the liability of the Guarantor hereunder shall be limited to the amount of £ _____ as a maximum liability and the Guarantor shall not be liable under this Guarantee for any greater or further amount.

2. The Guarantor agrees to remain fully bound on this Guarantee, notwithstanding any extension, forbearance, indulgence or waiver, or release or discharge or substitution of any party or collateral or security for the debt. In the event of default, the Creditor may seek payment directly from the Guarantor without need to proceed first against the Customer.

3. This Guarantee shall be binding upon and inure to the benefit of the parties, their successors and assigns.

IN WITNESS OF WHICH the parties have signed this agreement the day and year first above written.

_____
Signed by or on behalf of the Guarantor

_____
in the presence of (witness)

Name _____

Address _____

_____
Occupation _____

_____
Signed by or on behalf of the Creditor

_____
in the presence of (witness)

Name _____

Address _____

_____
Occupation _____

LIVING WILL

Name _____

Address _____

Date of birth _____

Doctor's details _____

National Health Number _____

I, _____, am of sound mind and make this Advance Directive now on my future medical care to my family, my doctors, other medical personnel and anyone else to whom it is relevant, for a time when, for reasons of physical or mental incapacity, I am unable to make my views known.

MEDICAL TREATMENT I DO NOT WANT:

I REFUSE medical procedures to prolong my life or keep me alive by artificial means if:

(1) I have a severe physical illness from which, in the opinion of _____ independent medical practitioners, it is unlikely that I will ever recover;

☐

or

(2) I have a severe mental illness which, in the opinion of _____ independent medical practitioners, has no likelihood of improvement and in addition I have a severe physical illness from which, in the opinion of _____ independent medical practitioners, it is unlikely that I will ever recover;

☐

or

(3) I am permanently unconscious and have been so for a period of at least ___ months and in the opinion of ___ independent medical practitioners there is no likelihood that I will ever recover.

☐

Medical treatment I DO want:

I DO wish to receive any medical treatment which will alleviate pain or distressing symptoms or will make me more comfortable. I accept that this may have the effect of shortening my life.

☐

If I am suffering from any of the conditions above and I am pregnant, I wish to RECEIVE medical procedures which will prolong my life or keep me alive by artificial means only until such time as my child has been safely delivered.

☐

Continued on next page

HEALTH CARE PROXY

I wish to appoint _____ of_____
_____ as my Health Care Proxy. S/he should be involved in any decisions about my health care options if I am physically or mentally unable to make my views known. I wish to make it clear that s/he is fully aware of my wishes and I request that his/her decisions be respected.

ADDITIONAL DIRECTIONS ON FUTURE HEALTH CARE

_____
_____
_____
_____
_____
_____
_____
_____

SIGNATURES

Signature _____ Date_____

Witness' signature _____ Date_____

I confirm that my views are still as stated above.

	Date	Signature	Witness' signature
1)	_____	_____	_____
2)	_____	_____	_____
3)	_____	_____	_____
4)	_____	_____	_____

116

LOAN AGREEMENT

THIS AGREEMENT IS MADE the _____ day of _____ 19 _____
BETWEEN:

(1) _____ (the "Borrower"); and

(2) _____ (the "Lender").

NOW IT IS HEREBY AGREED as follows:

1. **Loan**: Subject to and in accordance with this agreement, its terms, conditions and covenants the Lender agrees to lend to the Borrower on _____ 19_____ (the "Loan Date") the principal sum of _____ Pounds (£_____) (the "Loan").

2. **Note**: The Loan shall be evidenced by a Note in the form attached hereto as Exhibit A (the "Note") executed by the Borrower and delivered to the Lender on the Loan Date.

3. **Interest**: The Loan shall bear interest on the unpaid principal at an annual rate of _____ _____ percent (_____%). In the event of a default in payment the aforesaid interest rate shall apply to the total of principal and interest due at the time of default.

4. **Payment**: Payment shall be in accordance with the terms contained in the Note. The Note may, at any time and from time to time, be paid or prepaid in whole or in part without premium or penalty, except that any partial prepayment shall be (a) in multiples of £_____, (b) a minimum of £_____, applied to any instalments due under the Note in the inverse order of their maturity. Upon the payment of the outstanding principal in full or all of the instalments, if any, the interest on the Loan shall be computed and a final adjustment and payment of interest shall be made within five (5) days of the receipt of notice. Interest shall be calculated on the basis of a year of _____ days and the actual number of days elapsed.

5. **Security**: The Borrower agrees to secure the repayment of the Loan by executing those security documents attached hereto as Exhibit B (the "Security Documents") and shall deliver the Security Documents on the Loan Date. From time to time the Lender may demand, and the Borrower shall execute, additional loan documents which are reasonably necessary to perfect the Lender's security interests.

6. **Representations and Warranties**: The Borrower represents and warrants: (i) that the execution, delivery and performance of this agreement, and the Note and Security Documents have been duly authorised and are proper; (ii) that the financial statement submitted to the Lender fairly presents the financial condition of the Borrower as of the date of this agreement knowing that the Lender has relied thereon in granting the Loan; (iii) that the Borrower has no contingent obligations not disclosed or reserved against in said financial statement, and at the present time there are no material, unrealised or anticipated losses from any present commitment of the Borrower; (iv) that there will be no material adverse changes in the financial condition of the Borrower at the time of the Loan Date; (v) that the Borrower will advise the Lender of material adverse changes which occur at any time prior to the Loan Date and thereafter to the date of final payment; and (vi) that the Borrower has good and valid title to all of the property given as security hereunder. The Borrower represents and warrants that such representations and warranties shall be deemed to be continuing representations and warranties during the entire life of this agreement.

117

7. **Default**: The Borrower shall be in default: (i) if any payment due hereunder is not made within _____ (___) days of the date due; (ii) in the event of assignment by the Borrower for the benefit of creditors; (iii) upon the filing of any voluntary or involuntary petition for bankruptcy by or against the Borrower; or (iv) if the Borrower has breached any representation or warranty specified in this agreement.

8. **Governing Law:** This agreement, the Note(s) and the Security Documents shall be governed by, construed and enforced in accordance with the law of England and Wales to the jurisdiction of which the parties hereto submit.

IN WITNESS OF WHICH the parties have signed this agreement the day and year first above written.

_____   _____
Signed by or on behalf of the Borrower   Signed by or on behalf of the Lender

_____   _____
in the presence of (witness)   in the presence of (witness)

Name _____   Name _____

Address _____   Address _____

_____   _____
Occupation   Occupation

EXHIBIT A

Attach a copy of the Note

EXHIBIT B

Attach copies of the Security Documents

LOAN NOTE (LONG FORM)

THIS DEED IS MADE the _____ day of _____ 19 _____

BETWEEN:

(1) _____ of _____ (the "Borrower"); and

(2) _____ of _____ (the "Lender").

NOW THIS DEED WITNESSES as follows:

1. The Borrower hereby promises to pay to the order of the Lender the sum of _____ _____ Pounds (£_____), together with interest thereon at the rate of _____% per annum on the unpaid balance. The said amount shall be paid in the following manner:

_____

_____

2. All payments shall be first applied to interest and the balance to principal. This note may be prepaid, at any time, in whole or in part, without penalty.

3. This note shall at the option of any holder thereof be immediately due and payable upon the occurrence of any of the following:

(a) Failure of the Borrower to make any payment due hereunder within _____ days of its due date.

(b) Breach of any condition of any mortgage, loan agreement, or guarantee granted as collateral security for this note.

(c) Breach of any condition of any loan agreement or mortgage, if any, having a priority over any loan agreement or mortgage on security granted, in whole or in part, as collateral security for this note.

(d) Upon the death, incapacity, dissolution, receivership, insolvency or liquidation of either of the parties hereto, or any endorser or guarantor of this note.

4. In the event this note shall be in default and placed for collection, then the Borrower agrees to pay all reasonable solicitors fees and costs of collection. Payments not made within five (5) days of the due date shall be subject to a charge of _____ % per annum of the sum due. All payments hereunder shall be made to such address as may from time to time be designated by any party.

5. The undersigned and all other parties to this note, whether as endorsers, guarantors or sureties, agree to remain fully bound until this note shall be fully paid and further agree to remain bound, notwithstanding any extension, modification, waiver, or other indulgence or discharge or release of the Borrower hereunder or exchange, substitution, or release of any collateral security granted as security for this note. No variation or waiver by any holder hereof shall be binding unless in writing; and any waiver on any one occasion shall not be a waiver for any other or future occasion. Any variation or change in terms hereunder granted by any holder hereof, shall be valid and binding upon each of the undersigned, notwithstanding the acknowledgement of any of the undersigned.

IN WITNESS OF WHICH the parties have signed this deed the day and year first above written.

Signed by or on behalf of the First Party

---
in the presence of (witness)

Name

Address

Occupation

Signed by or on behalf of the Second Party

---
in the presence of (witness)

Name

Address

Occupation

LOAN NOTE (SHORT FORM)

THIS DEED is made the _____ day of _____ 19_____

BY:

_____ of _____ (the "Borrower").

WHEREAS:

The Borrower is indebted to _____ (the "Lender") in the sum

of £ _____.

NOW THIS DEED WITNESSES as follows:

1.   The Borrower promises to pay to the order of the Lender the sum of _____
_____ Pounds (£ _____), with annual interest of _____ % on any unpaid
balance.

2.   This note shall be paid in _____ consecutive and equal instalments of £ _____
each with the first payment one _____ from date hereof, and the same amount on the
same day of each _____ thereafter, provided the entire principal balance and any
accrued but unpaid interest shall be fully paid on or before _____ 19_____.

3.   This note may be prepaid without penalty. All payments shall be first applied to interest
and the balance to principal.

4.   This note shall be due and payable upon demand by any holder hereof should the
Borrower default in any payment beyond _____ days of its due date.

IN WITNESS OF WHICH the Borrower has executed this deed the day and year first above
written.

_____
Signed by or on behalf of the Debtor

_____
in the presence of (witness)

Name _____

Address _____

_____

Occupation _____

LOAN PAYMENT RECORD

Borrower: _____ Creditor: _____

Terms: _____

Date Due	Date Paid	Amount	Balance
_____	_____	£ _____	£ _____
_____	_____	£ _____	£ _____
_____	_____	£ _____	£ _____
_____	_____	£ _____	£ _____
_____	_____	£ _____	£ _____
_____	_____	£ _____	£ _____
_____	_____	£ _____	£ _____
_____	_____	£ _____	£ _____
_____	_____	£ _____	£ _____
_____	_____	£ _____	£ _____
_____	_____	£ _____	£ _____
_____	_____	£ _____	£ _____
_____	_____	£ _____	£ _____
_____	_____	£ _____	£ _____
_____	_____	£ _____	£ _____
_____	_____	£ _____	£ _____
_____	_____	£ _____	£ _____
_____	_____	£ _____	£ _____
_____	_____	£ _____	£ _____
_____	_____	£ _____	£ _____
_____	_____	£ _____	£ _____
_____	_____	£ _____	£ _____

LODGER/BED & BREAKFAST LICENCE
(for a Room in a Furnished House)

The PROPERTY _____

_____

The ROOM means the room at the Property which has been agreed between the Licensor and Licensee to

be taken by the Licensee

The LICENSOR _____

_____ whose address is the Property above

The LICENSEE _____

_____

The PERIOD _____ weeks/months* beginning on _____

(delete paragraph
if not required)

⌈Subject to the right for either party at any time during the Period to end this Agreement⌉ (* delete as appropriate)

⌊earlier by giving to the other written notice of _____ week(s)/month(s)*⌋

The SERVICES means the services that the Licensor hereby agrees to provide to the Licensor being to

[clean the Room and Property] [provide clean sheets] [provide breakfast] [provide dinner]*

The PAYMENT £ _____ per week/month* payable in advance on the _____ of each week/month*

being payment for the Room and Services

The DEPOSIT £_____

The INVENTORY means the list of the Licensor's possessions at the Property which has been signed by the

Licensor and the Licensee

DATED _____

SIGNED _____   _____

_____(The Licensor)_____   _____(The Licensee)_____

THIS AGREEMENT comprises the particulars detailed above and the terms and conditions printed overleaf whereby the Room is licensed by the Licensor and taken by the Licensee for occupation during the Period upon making the Payment.

Terms and Conditions on next page

LODGER/BED & BREAKFAST LICENCE
Terms & Conditions

1. The Licensee will:

1.1 only in conjunction with the occupation of the Room be allowed to share with the other occupiers of the Property the use and facilities of the common parts of the Property (including such bathroom, toilet, kitchen and sitting room facilities as may be at the Property)

1.2 pay the Payment at the times and in the manner aforesaid without any deduction or abatement of set-off whatsoever

1.3 keep the interior of the Room in a good clean and tenantable state and condition and not damage or injure the Property or any part of it and if at the end of the period any item on the Inventory requires repair, replacing, cleaning or laundering the Licensee will pay for the same (reasonable wear and tear and damage by insured risks excepted)

1.4 maintain in the Room and keep in a good and clean condition all of the items listed in the Inventory

1.5 not make any alteration or addition to the Room nor without the Licensor's prior written consent to do any redecoration or painting of the Room

1.6 not do or omit to do anything on or at the Property which may be or become a nuisance or annoyance to the Licensor or any other occupiers of the Property or owners or occupiers of adjoining or nearby premises or which may in any way prejudice the insurance of the Property or cause an increase in the premium payable therefor

1.7 not without the Licensor's prior consent allow or keep any pet or any kind of animal at the Property

1.8 not use or occupy the Room in any way whatsoever other than as a private residence

1.9 not part with or share possession or occupation of the Room or any part thereof

1.10 pay interest at the rate of 4% above the Base Lending Rate for the time being of the Licensor's bankers upon any payment or other money due from the Licensee under this Agreement which is more than 3 days in arrear in respect of the period from when it become due down to the date of payment

2. In the event of the Payment being unpaid for more than 10 days after it is due (whether demanded or not) or there being a breach of any other of the Licensee's obligations under this Agreement then the Licensor may re-enter the Room and this Agreement shall thereupon determine absolutely but without prejudice to any of the Licensor's other rights and remedies in respect of any outstanding obligations on the part of the Licensee

3. The Deposit has been paid by the Licensee and is held by the Licensor to secure compliance with the Licensee's obligations under this Agreement (without prejudice to the Licensor's other rights and remedies) and if, at any time during the Period, the Licensor is obliged to draw upon it to satisfy any outstanding breaches of such obligations then the Licensee shall forthwith make such additional payment as is necessary to restore the full amount of the Deposit held by the Licensor. As soon as reasonably practicable following determination of this Agreement the Licensor shall return to the Licensee the Deposit or the balance thereof after any deductions properly made

4. The Licensor will insure the Property and the items listed on the Inventory

5. The Licensor hereby notifies the Licensee that any notices (including notices in proceedings) should be served upon the Licensor at the address stated with the name of the Licensor overleaf

6. In the event of damage to or destruction of the Property by any of the risks insured against by the Licensor the Licensee shall be relieved from making the Payment to the extent that the Licensee's use and enjoyment of the Property is thereby prevented and from performance of its obligations as to the state and condition of the Property to the extent of and whilst there prevails any such damage or destruction (except to the extent that the insurance is prejudiced by any act or default of the Licensee) the amount in case of dispute to be settled by arbitration.

7. So long as the reference to a right of early termination in the definition of "the PERIOD" overleaf (the "early termination right") has not been deleted then either party may at an time during the period terminate this Agreement by giving to the other prior written notice to that effect, the length of such notice to be that stated in the early termination right, and upon the expiry of said notice this Agreement shall end with no further liability for either party save for any antecedent breach

8. The Licensee shall not have exclusive possession of the Room and the identity of the other occupiers of the Property shall be in the absolute discretion of the Licensor

9. Where the context so admits:

9.1 the "Property" includes all of the Licensor's fixtures and fittings at or upon the Property and all of the items listed in the Inventory and (for the avoidance of doubt) the Room

9.2 the "Period" shall mean the period stated in the particulars overleaf or any shorter or longer period in the event of an earlier termination or an extension or holding over respectively

10. All references to the singular shall include the plural and vice versa and any obligations or liabilities of more than one person shall be joint and several and an obligation on the part of a party shall include an obligation not to allow or permit the breach of that obligation

124

LOST CREDIT CARD NOTICE

Date _____

To _____

_____

_____

Dear _____

This is to confirm that the credit card described below has been lost or stolen. Please put an immediate stop on all credit in respect of the card. I last remember using the card myself on _____ 19___ at _____. I shall destroy the card if subsequently found, and I should be grateful if you would issue me a replacement card.

Yours faithfully

_____
Cardholder

Name _____

Address _____

_____

Tel. _____

_____
Credit Card Number

LOST LUGGAGE COMPENSATION REQUEST

Date _____

To _____

_____

_____

Ref Flight No. _____

Dear _____

I took the above flight on _____ from _____ to _____.
After I arrived at _____ airport I notified your staff of the non-appearance of
my luggage and filled out and submitted a report as requested. It has now been _____
days since then and I have not received any response from you.

Under the terms of the Warsaw Convention I am legally entitled to compensation for the loss
of my luggage. The current rate is £13.63 per kilogram of lost luggage, as laid down in the
Convention; at check-in my luggage weighed ___ kg, and I therefore claim £_____.

I look forward to hearing from you shortly with any news of my luggage or your offer of compensation.

Yours sincerely

_____

Name _____

Address _____

_____

Tel. _____

MAGAZINE ARTICLE ROYALTY CONTRACT

THIS AGREEMENT IS MADE the _____ day of _____ 19____

BETWEEN:

(1) _____ (the "Author"); and

(2) _____ (the "Publisher").

NOW IT IS HEREBY AGREED as follows:

1. The Author agrees to deliver an original and one copy of the manuscript which is tentatively titled _____ (the "Work"), to the Publisher on or before _____ 19 _____. The Work is described as:

_____

_____

If the Author fails to deliver the Work within _____ days of the Work due date, the Publisher may terminate this contract.

2. Within _____ days of receipt of the Work, the Publisher agrees to notify the Author if the Publisher finds the work unsatisfactory in form or content. The Publisher also agrees to provide the Author with a list of necessary changes. The Author agrees to make the changes within _____ days. If the Publisher still reasonably rejects the Work as unsatisfactory, the Publisher may terminate this contract.

3. The Author grants the Publisher the first _____ Serial Rights in the Work. Any rights not specifically granted to the Publisher shall remain with the Author. The Author agrees not to exercise any retained rights in such a manner as to adversely affect the value of the rights granted to the Publisher.

4. The Publisher shall pay to the Author upon acceptance of the Work the amount of £_____.

5. The style, format, design, layout, and any required editorial changes of the published work shall be in the sole discretion of the Publisher.

6. The Author warrants that:
    (a) the Work is the sole creation of the Author;
    (b) the Author is the sole owner of the rights granted under this contract;
    (c) the Work does not infringe the copyright of any other work;
    (d) the Work is original and has not been published before;
    (e) the Work is not in the public domain;
    (f) the Work is not obscene, libellous, and does not invade the privacy of any person;
    (g) all statements of fact in the Work are true and based upon reasonable research.

7.   The Publisher acknowledges that the Author retains worldwide copyright in the Work.

8.   The Publisher agrees that, within one year from the receipt of a satisfactory manuscript of the Work, the Work will be published at Publisher's sole expense. If the Publisher fails to do so, unless prevented by conditions beyond the Publisher's control, the Author may terminate this Contract.

9.   This contract is the complete agreement between the Author and Publisher. No modification or waiver of any terms will be valid unless in writing and signed by both parties.

IN WITNESS OF WHICH the parties have signed this agreement the day and year first above written.

_____

Signed by the Author

_____

in the presence of (witness)

Name _____

Address _____

_____

Occupation _____

_____

Signed for and on behalf of the Publisher

_____

in the presence of (witness)

Name _____

Address _____

_____

Occupation _____

MAIL-ORDER GOODS REJECTION

Date _____

To _____

_____

_____

Dear Sirs

On _____ I ordered the following item(s) listed in your _____ mail order catalogue: _____.

I received these goods on _____. However, I am not happy with it/them for the following reason(s):

[The goods are not of satisfactory quality, because of the following serious defects: _____.]

[The goods do not match their description in the catalogue, because: _____.]

[The goods are not reasonably fit for their purpose, because: _____.]

Under the Sale of Goods Act 1979 as amended by the Sale and Supply of Goods Act 1994 you are in breach of contract and I am legally entitled to a full refund of the purchase price, plus the cost of postage and packing. Please send me a cheque for £ _____ within 10 days and advise me what you would like me to do with the goods. If you do not reimburse me I will have no alternative but to issue a county court summons without further notice.

Yours sincerely

_____

Name _____

Address _____

_____

Tel. _____

MAILING LIST REMOVAL REQUEST

Date _____

To The Mailing Preference Service

Freepost 22

London W1E 7EZ

Dear Sirs

I regularly receive unsolicited, 'junk' mail from companies advertising their products.

I understand I can ask you to have my name and this household removed from the mailing lists of companies who send out unsolicited mail and that this service is free of charge.

Please put this into action with immediate effect.

Yours faithfully

Name _____

Address _____

_____

_____

_____

MATERNITY ABSENCE RETURN NOTICE

Date _____

To _____

_____

_____

Dear _____

As required, I am writing to you at least 21 days before I exercise my right to return to work from my maternity absence.

I intend to return to work on _____ 19____.

Yours sincerely

_____

MATERNITY LEAVE AND MATERNITY ABSENCE NOTICE

Date _____

To _____

_____

_____

Dear _____

This is to inform you that I am pregnant and wish to take both maternity leave and maternity absence. I understand that I have completed a sufficient period of continuous employment with you to be entitled to maternity absence. I enclose a medical/maternity certificate date _____ 199____ from Dr. _____.

The expected week of childbirth is _____ and I intend to start taking my maternity leave on _____ 19____. I understand that I am entitled to 14 weeks' maternity leave, and thereafter maternity absence until the end of the 28th week after the week in which I give birth. I intend to exercise the right to return to work after that date.

I wish also to receive the Statutory Maternity Pay to which I am entitled during my maternity leave.

Yours sincerely

_____

MATERNITY LEAVE EARLY RETURN REQUEST

Date _____

To _____

_____

_____

Dear _____

This is to inform you that I intend to return to work before the end of my maternity leave period and I am giving you at least seven days notice as required by law.

I intend to return to work on _____ 19____.

Yours sincerely

_____

MATERNITY LEAVE NOTICE

Date _____

To _____

_____

_____

Dear _____

This is to inform you that I am pregnant and wish to take maternity leave. I enclose a medical/ maternity certificate dated _____ 19 ___ from Dr. _____.

The expected week of childbirth is _____ and I intend to start taking my maternity leave on _____ 19 ___. I understand that I am entitled to 14 weeks' leave in total by law.

Please also let me know if I am entitled to receive Statutory Maternity Pay during my maternity leave.

Yours sincerely

_____

MEDICAL RECORDS REQUEST

Date _____

To _____

_____

_____

Ref _____

Dear Dr _____

I am writing because I would like to see my medical records.

As you are no doubt aware, I am entitled under the Patient's Charter to see and receive any of my medical records on paper, whether typed or handwritten, made on or after 1 November 1991, while the Data Protection Act 1984 allows me to see my records kept on computer.

As my records have been updated within the last 40 days, after my visit to your surgery on _____, I understand there will be no charge for having access to my records, but that you may make a charge for providing me with a copy of them.

Please also confirm whether you would be able to go through my records with me. I look forward to hearing from you within three weeks with a date on which I can see my records.

Yours sincerely

_____

Name _____

Address _____

_____

Tel. _____

MODEL RELEASE

In consideration for the sum of £ _____, receipt of which I hereby acknowledge, I grant to

_____

the exclusive world rights, including copyright, to use any photographs containing my image for publication in _____ and for subsidiary use, promotional use, future revisions and future editions of the same.

I waive any right to inspect or approve the final use of such photographs and I waive any right to file any legal actions, including libel or invasion of privacy, based on any use of the photographs under this release.

I am of legal age and understand the content of this document.

Permission is granted on _____ 19____.

_____
Signature of Model

MUTUAL CANCELLATION OF CONTRACT

THIS AGREEMENT IS MADE the _____ day of _____ 19 ____

BETWEEN:

(1) _____ of _____ (the "First Party"); and

(2) _____ of _____ (the "Second Party").

WHEREAS:

(A) The parties entered into a Contract dated _____ 19 ____ (the "Contract").

(B) The parties wish mutually to terminate the Contract and all their obligations and rights thereunder.

NOW IT IS HEREBY AGREED as follows:

1. The parties hereby agree to terminate the Contract.

2. The parties further agree that the termination shall be without further recourse by either party against the other and this document shall constitute mutual releases of any further obligations under the Contract, all to the same extent as if the Contract had not been entered into in the first instance, provided the parties shall herewith undertake to perform the act, if any, described below to terminate the Contract, which obligations, shall remain binding, notwithstanding this agreement to cancel.

_____

_____

IN WITNESS OF WHICH the parties have signed this agreement the day and year first above written.

_____ _____
Signed by or on behalf of the First Party   Signed by or on behalf of the Second Party

_____ _____
in the presence of (witness)   in the presence of (witness)

Name _____   Name _____

Address _____   Address _____

_____ _____
Occupation   Occupation

MUTUAL RELEASES

THIS AGREEMENT IS MADE the _____ day of _____ 19 ____

BETWEEN:

(1) _____ of _____ (the "First Party"); and

(2) _____ of _____ (the "Second Party").

NOW IT IS HEREBY AGREED as follows:

1. The First Party and the Second Party do hereby completely, mutually and reciprocally release, discharge, acquit and forgive each other from all claims, contracts, actions, demands, agreements, liabilities, and proceedings of every nature and description that either party has or may have against the other, arising from the beginning of time to the date of these presents, including but not necessarily limited to an incident or claim described as:

_____

_____

_____

2. This release shall be binding upon and inure to the benefit of the parties, their successors and assigns.

IN WITNESS OF WHICH the parties have signed this agreement the day and year first above written.

_____   _____
Signed by or on behalf of the First Party   Signed by or on behalf of the Second Party

_____   _____
in the presence of (witness)   in the presence of (witness)

Name _____   Name _____

Address _____   Address _____

_____   _____
Occupation _____   Occupation _____

NANNY'S EMPLOYMENT CONTRACT

DATED _____

BETWEEN (1) _____ of _____

                        _____ (the 'Employer');

and

        (2) _____ of _____

                        _____ (the 'Employee').

NOW IT IS AGREED as follows:

1. JOB TITLE AND PLACE OF WORK. The Employer agrees to employ the Employee from _____ 199____ in the capacity of nanny to _____ (the 'Children') at _____(the 'Home') and for limited periods wherever holidays are taken, both in and outside the UK.

2. REMUNERATION. The Employer shall pay the Employee a salary of £_____ per week net payable monthly in arrears after deduction of income tax and national insurance.

3. HOURS OF WORK. The Employee's normal hours of work shall be _____ to _____ on Mondays to Fridays. The Employee will also be expected to work ___ weekends per month (within the working hours stated above), plus babysitting as set out in Clause 5 below.

4. OVERTIME. Overtime will be paid at the rate of £___ per hour.

5. BABYSITTING. The Employee will babysit on ___ evenings of each month, to be agreed in advance with the Employer.

6. HOLIDAYS. The Employee shall be entitled to _____ working days' holiday per calendar year at full pay in addition to the normal public holidays. Holidays must be taken at a time that is convenient to the Employer with a minimum notification period of ____ weeks and no more than _____ weeks' holiday may be taken at any one time.

7. SICKNESS. The Employee will take reasonable care to maintain good health. [In respect of sickness lasting more than 7 calendar days, the Employee must on the eighth calendar day of sickness provide a medical certificate stating the reason for absence and thereafter provide a certificate each week to cover any subsequent period of absence]. The Employee will be paid her normal basic remuneration for ____ days in any one sick pay year which runs from _____ to _____. Thereafter, the Employee will be entitled to Statutory Sick Pay, the qualifying days for which will be Monday to Friday.

8. ACCOMMODATION. The Employee will have her own bedroom [with personal television] [and telephone]. All household expenditure including food and services will be paid for by the Employer. The Employee will be responsible for cleaning her room and will be expected to ensure its cleanliness and tidy presentation at all times.

9. FACILITIES. The Employee will afford the Employer reasonable privacy at all times where appropriate. It is understood that the Employer will have priority at all times.

10. TELEPHONE. The Employee [will have her own telephone line and will be responsible for paying all call charges; the Employer will meet all line rental charges][will have use of the Employer's telephone, subject to any restrictions discussed with the Employer].

11. DUTIES. The Employee's duties are as listed on the Job Description which forms part of this Agreement, but these duties may vary on occasions as circumstances require.

12. PROBATIONARY PERIOD. During an initial probationary period of 2 weeks either party may terminate this Agreement without notice.

Continued on next page

13. TERMINATION. During the first _____ weeks of employment, _____ week's written notice is required on either side. After _____ weeks' continuous employment, either the Employer or the Employee may terminate this Agreement by giving _____ weeks' written notice.

14. CONFIDENTIALITY. It is a condition of employment that the Employee now and at all times in the future, save as may be required by law, keeps secret all the private and commercial concerns of the Employer and of the Employer's household.

15. PENSION. The Employer [does][does not] operate a Pension Scheme. Details are attached is applicable.

16. DISCIPLINE. Reasons that will give rise to disciplinary action against the Employee will include:

1. Causing a disruptive influence in the household

2. Job incompetence

3. Unsatisfactory standard of dress or appearance

4. Conduct during or outside working hours prejudicial to the interests or reputation of the Employer.

5. Unreliability in time-keeping or attendance.

6. Failure to comply with instructions, procedures and House Rules.

7. Breach of confidentiality clause.

In the event of the need to take disciplinary action the procedure shall be:

(a) Oral warning

(b) Written warning

(c) Dismissal

Reasons which might give rise to immediate dismissal include the following:

(i) Theft

(ii) Drunkenness

(iii) Drug taking or trafficking

(iv) Lying

(v) Endangering the lives of the children

17. HOUSE RULES:

1. The Employee shall not entertain male acquaintances in the home.

2. No friends or acquaintances of the Employee may stay overnight.

3. Under no circumstances may any friends or acquaintances be left alone in the home with or without the children or be given a house key.

4. The Employee shall dress appropriately for work

5. The Employee and any visitors may not smoke in the home at any time.

6. The Employee may not drink alcohol during working hours.

7. The Employee may have no more than two friends in the home when babysitting.

8. The Employee must be home by midnight during the week.

SIGNED _____   SIGNED _____
       by the Employer   by the Employee

NANNY JOB DESCRIPTION

Daily duties

1. Providing for the children's physical needs including feeding, bathing, dressing and changing. Maintaining routine and ensuring proper rests each day.

2. Washing, ironing and maintaining the children's clothes, personal effects, equipment and toys.

3. Preparing food and drink for the children in consultation with the Employer and leaving food and drink so that it is available for parents and others to to feed during off-duty periods.

4. Maintaining a high standard of order and cleanliness in the nursery, bathroom and in own room.

5. Setting out and clearing away play activities both in the nursery and elsewhere as necessary. Leaving house tidy at the end of the day.

6. Maintaining changing bags so that they are fully stocked.

General duties

1. Exercising full control of the children's behaviour during duty.

2. Promoting the children's physical, social and emotional development including organising suitable activities for the children in consultation with the employers.

3. Promoting the children's sensory and intellectual development.

4. Promoting the development of the children's language and communication skills.

5. Observing and assessing the development and behaviour of the children.

6. Maintaining a happy and child-orientated environment.

7. Maintaining and ensuring the children's safety.

8. Administering medication in consultation with the Employer.

9. 'Mucking in' with family life, i.e. setting dishwasher off, helping with washing up, etc.

Other duties

1. Keeping a petty-cash book, retaining receipts and accounting for relevant expenditure within any budget that may be agreed.

2. Shopping, managing and maintaining stocks of the children's requirements, relating to necessary food, drink, toiletries, etc. using delivery services where cost-effective. Helping with general household shopping.

3. Attending necessary visits to medical practitioners as and when appropriate.

4. Advising parents and researching details about purchases of nursery furniture, equipment and clothing and organising purchases.

5. Being responsible for drying family laundry.

NATIONAL LOTTERY SYNDICATE AGREEMENT

SYNDICATE NAME: _____

MANAGER	DATE OF APPOINTMENT	SIGNATURE

MEMBER	INDIVIDUAL STAKE (to be paid IN ADVANCE of each Draw by the agreed deadline)	DATE JOINED SYNDICATE	MANAGER'S SIGNATURE	MEMBER'S SIGNATURE	DATE LEFT SYNDICATE	MANAGER'S SIGNATURE

The Syndicate will participate in Draws on: Wednesdays only*   (*delete as appropriate)

Saturdays only*

Wednesdays and Saturdays*

Agreed deadline for payment of Individual Stakes: Day (each week):_____

Time: _____

Syndicate Rules on next page

NATIONAL LOTTERY SYNDICATE RULES

1. Definitions

'**Draw**' means a draw of the Camelot National Lottery in which the Syndicate has agreed to participate;

'**Individual Stake**' means the stake payable by each Member as set out in this Agreement and received by the Manager in advance of each Draw by the agreed deadline;

'**Manager**' means the Manager of the Syndicate, who shall be appointed and may be replaced at any time without notice by a majority of the Members;

'**Members**' means all those persons who have joined and not left the Syndicate;

'**Syndicate Stake**' means the total of the Members' Individual Stakes in respect of any Draw.

2. Manager's Responsibilities

2.1 The Manager will:

    (a) establish a procedure for agreeing the combinations of numbers to be entered by the Syndicate for each Draw;

    (b) buy tickets bearing the agreed numbers for the amount of the Syndicate Stake for each Draw. However, if the Syndicate Stake is not sufficient to buy tickets bearing all agreed combinations of numbers in any Draw, the Manager shall have absolute discretion as to which of the agreed combinations to enter;

    (c) collect any prize money and account to the Members for it in proportion to their Individual Stakes, holding it in trust for the Members in the meantime.

2.2 If any Member fails to pay his Individual Stake to the Manager in advance of any Draw by the agreed deadline, the Manager may (but shall not be obliged to) pay that Individual Stake on the Member's behalf and, if the Manager does so, the Member will reimburse the Manager forthwith upon demand.

2.3 The Manager shall not be liable to any Member for any loss or damage arising out of any failing of the Manager under this Agreement, provided that the Manager has acted honestly.

3. Members' Responsibilities

The Members will each pay their Individual Stake to the Manager in advance of each Draw by the agreed deadline.

4. Ceasing to be a Member

A Member shall be removed from the Group:

4.1 if the Member wishes to leave; or

4.2 at the discretion of the Manager, if the Member fails to pay his Individual Stake in accordance with Rule 3 in respect of any 3 weeks (whether consecutive or non-consecutive); or

4.3 at the discretion of the Manager, if the Member fails to reimburse the Manager in accordance with Rule 2.2.

5. This Agreement

5.1 It shall be the responsibility of the Manager to update and amend this Agreement. Any such amendment, other than the removal of a Member in accordance with Rule 4, must have been authorised by majority vote of the Members.

5.2 The list of Members in this Agreement shall be conclusive as to the membership of the Syndicate at any point in time, provided that a person whose application for membership has been accepted by the Manager and who has duly paid an agreed Individual Stake shall not be excluded from a share of prize money under Rule 2.1(c) merely because the Agreement has not been updated to record that person as a Member.

5.3 The appointment or replacement of the Manager shall take effect whether or not this Agreement has been amended to that effect.

NEIGHBOURS: ANTI-SOCIAL COUNCIL TENANTS COMPLAINT

Date _____

To The Environmental Health Officer

_____ Local Authority

_____

Dear Sir

I understand that under the Housing Act 1996 councils can opt to use new, swift powers of eviction to deal with troublesome local-authority housing tenants.

I should be grateful if you would confirm whether or not you have opted to use these powers and, if so, that you can act to deal with tenants who occupy the following property:_____
_____.

I speak both for myself and on behalf of neighbours when I say that these council tenants are consistently anti-social and are a nuisance for the following reasons:
_____
_____.

I look forward to hearing what course of action you will take.

Yours faithfully

_____

Name _____

Address _____

_____

Tel. _____

NEIGHBOURS: BOUNDARY DISPUTE

Date _____

To _____

_____

_____

Dear _____

Following our recent conversation about the boundary between our properties I am writing to confirm that I have checked [at the District Land Registry][the title deeds] and can advise you that the fence/wall in question belongs to _____.

The plans clearly indicate who is the owner of the fence/wall by the use of small 'T' marks on the side of the boundary to whom that boundary belongs. This would also confirm the our presumption that the fence belongs to the person on whose side its supporting posts are.

I trust this settles the matter.

Yours sincerely

_____

Name _____

Address _____

_____

Tel. _____

NEIGHBOURS: EXCESSIVE NOISE COMPLAINT

Date _____

To The Environmental Health Officer

               Local Authority
_____

_____

Dear Sir

I am writing to ask that you help in resolving my complaint with my neighbours_____

_____ of _____ .

My complaint is that they produce excessive and therefore unreasonable noise; it interferes with my enjoyment of the property to the extent that I find it intolerable. I have politely asked my neighbours to stop making so much noise, but to no effect. I have also obtained written statements from other affected neighbours to support my complaint, copies of which I am enclosing.

I understand that the Noise Act 1996 gives the council immediate powers to deal with high levels of noise from residential properties between the hours of 11pm and 7am. Considering it is often during the night that noise is excessive I trust you will be able to act quickly and decisively to put an end to it.

I look forward to hearing what course of action you will take.

Yours faithfully

_____

Name
_____

Address
_____

NEIGHBOURS: FAULTY CAR ALARM COMPLAINT

Date _____

To _____

_____

_____

Dear _____

I am writing to complain about the alarm of your _____ car, registration number _____, which frequently goes off without good cause for prolonged periods when the vehicle is unattended, causing considerable nuisance.

Under the Noise and Statutory Nuisance Act 1993 the local environmental health officer (EHO) can serve an abatement notice on the owner or driver of a car with a faulty alarm to remedy the fault. If the alarm goes off and after an hour the owner/driver has not been found the officer can immobilise the alarm or remove the vehicle.

This is to advise you that if your car's alarm continues to cause a nuisance I shall contact the EHO and request that action be taken.

Yours sincerely

_____

Name _____

Address _____

_____

Tel. _____

NEIGHBOURS: OVERHANGING TREE NOTICE

Date _____

To _____

_____

_____

Dear _____

I am writing to let you know that I intend to cut the branches of the _____ tree which overhangs my property from yours. My reasons for doing this are as follows:

_____.

I am legally entitled to do this at the point where the branches cross the boundary between our two properties, unless a Preservation Order protects this tree. I should be grateful if would confirm whether such an order exists. As we do not live in a conservation area I am not intending to ask the local council before cutting the tree.

Please let me know whether you would like the cut branches, to which you are legally entitled.

I look forward to hearing from you shortly.

Yours sincerely

_____

Name _____

Address _____

_____

Tel. _____

NEIGHBOURS: PROBLEM TREE ROOTS NOTICE

Date _____

To _____

_____

_____

Dear _____

I am writing to warn you that roots of the _____ tree growing in your garden are beginning to cause the following settlement damage to my property, as verified by the enclosed surveyor's report: _____.

I thought it wise to bring to your attention the fact that under law you are legally responsible for the damage done by your tree roots to my property. Please confirm whether or not you will undertake the work to (a) cut the roots back to the boundary that divides our properties and (b) repair the damage. Should you fail to do this I will employ a contractor myself and claim the costs from you, as I am legally entitled to do.

I look forward to hearing from you.

Yours sincerely

_____

Name _____

Address _____

_____

Tel. _____

NEIGHBOURS: RESIDENTS' PARKING CONTROL PETITION

Date _____

To The Highways Department

_____ Council

_____

Dear Sirs

I am writing on behalf of the residents of the _____ area to request that you impose residents parking control in the area. Over the past few years parking has become increasingly difficult for residents and a source of growing frustration. Judging by the beneficial effects on other areas, residents parking would greatly improve the situation and reduce the current congestion and pollution levels which are not helped by non-resident motorists who currently use our streets for parking in.

You will see that judging by the number of households that have signed the enclosed petition, the amount of support for a residents' parking scheme in this area is considerable. We all hope you will give this matter the consideration it deserves and that you will decide favourably.

I look forward to hearing from you.

Yours faithfully

_____

Name _____

Address _____

_____

Tel. _____

NEIGHBOURS: 'RIGHT TO LIGHT' NOTICE

Date _____

To _____

_____

_____

Dear _____

I am writing concerning the new extension you are planning to build onto your property.

You may not be aware that the window on the _____ floor of this building facing your property has enjoyed a certain level of light uninterrupted for over 20 years and, as a result, enjoys what's called a 'right to light' under law (and the title deeds do not prevent such a right from accruing). This means that the level of light the windows receive from the direction of your property is protected.

I feel I should warn you that should your extension substantially reduce the amount of light falling on this window I will take legal action through my solicitor.

Yours sincerely

_____

Name _____

Address _____

_____

Tel. _____

NEW CAR COMPLAINT

Date _____

To _____

_____

_____

Ref _____

Dear _____

I purchased a _____ (year, make, model, engine size) from your dealership on _____. On _____ I discovered the car had the following fault:_____.

Under Section 14 of the amended Sale of Goods Act 1979 (as amended by the Sale & Supply of Goods Act 1994) the car should have been of 'satisfactory quality' when sold. The fact that the car developed a fault only _____ days after purchase proves that the car was inherently faulty at the time of purchase, which constitutes your breach of contract, not the manufacturer's.

I therefore request that you [repair the car free of charge, whilst reserving my rights under the above Act][collect the car from me and refund the purchase price in full] as I am legally entitled to do.

I look forward to hearing from you very shortly.

Yours sincerely

_____

Name _____

Address _____

_____

Tel. _____

NOMINATION OF REPLACEMENT ROOM
(House/Flat Share Agreement)

Date _____

Ref _____

To _____

_____

_____

Dear Sharer(s)

Re. _____

Our Agreement in respect of your Room at the above Property states that you may be required to move to another room in the Property if required by me/us. Please note that I/we do now wish to move you from the Room you currently occupy to another room in the Property and which is located at

_____

and would ask that you make the move into this new Room straight away.

Thanking you in anticipation for your co-operation in this.

Yours sincerely

_____

_____

_____

_____

NOTICE OF ASSIGNMENT

Date _____

To _____

_____

_____

Ref _____

Dear _____

I attach a copy of an assignment dated _____ 19 _____ by which I assigned my interest in the contract referred to therein to _____ of _____ (the "Assignee"). Please hold all sums of money affected by such assignment, now or hereafter in your possession, that otherwise are payable to me under the terms of our original agreement, for the benefit of the Assignee, in accordance with the provisions of the assignment.

Yours sincerely

_____

Name _____

Address _____

_____

Tel. _____

NOTICE TO TERMINATE

(Rental Agreement or
House/Flat Share Agreement)

TO _____ (name(s) of
Tenant/Sharer)
_____

**YOUR
LANDLORD/
OWNER** _____ (name(s) and
address of
Landlord/Owner)
_____
_____

**REQUIRES
POSSESSION OF
THE PROPERTY
KNOWN AS** _____ (address of the
Property)
_____

ON THE _____ (Date for
Possession)

SIGNED BY _____ (the Landlord/
Owner **or** his/her
agent)
(if signed by the agent then the agent's name and address must
also be written here) _____
_____
_____

DATE OF NOTICE _____

IMPORTANT NOTICE TO LANDLORDS/OWNERS:

In the case of an Assured Shorthold Tenancy Rental Agreement the Date for Possession must be at least TWO MONTHS after the Tenant receives this Notice and in the case of a House/Flat Share Agreement (Non-Resident Owner) it must be at least FOUR WEEKS after the Sharer receives this Notice; in the case of a House/Flat Share Agreement (Resident Owner) ANY REASONABLE PERIOD of notice can be given.

IMPORTANT NOTICE :

(1) If the Tenant/Sharer does not leave the dwelling, the Landlord/Owner must get an order for possession from the court before the Tenant/Sharer can lawfully be evicted. The Landlord/Owner cannot apply for such an order before the Notice to Terminate has run out, i.e. the Date for Possession.

(2) A Tenant/Sharer who does not know if he has any right to remain in possession after the Notice to Terminate runs out can obtain advice from a solicitor. Help with all or part of the cost of legal advice and assistance may be available under the Legal Aid Scheme. The Tenant/Sharer should also be able to obtain information from a Citizens Advice Bureau, a Housing Aid Centre or a rent officer.

NOTICE TO TERMINATE
(House/Flat Share Agreement)

THIS NOTICE TO
BE GIVEN BY
SHARERS

TO _____ (name(s) and
_____ address of
_____ Owner)

I/WE _____ (name(s) of
_____ Sharer)

**GIVE YOU
NOTICE THAT
OUR AGREEMENT
IN RESPECT OF** _____ (address of the
_____ Property)

**IS HEREBY
TERMINATED
WITH EFFECT
FROM THE** _____ (Date for Posses-
sion)

SIGNED BY _____ (the Sharer(s))

DATE OF NOTICE _____

IMPORTANT NOTICE TO SHARERS:

In the case of a House/Flat Share Agreement (Non-Resident Owner) the Date For Possession must be at least FOUR WEEKS after the Owner receives this Notice and in the case of a House/Flat Share Agreement (Resident Owner) ANY REASONABLE PERIOD of notice can be given.

* An Assured Shorthold Tenancy Rental Agreement needs NO NOTICE from the Tenant at the end of the Agreement.

IMPORTANT NOTICE :

(1) If the Tenant/Sharer does not leave the dwelling, the Landlord/Owner must get an order for possession from the court before the Tenant/Sharer can lawfully be evicted. The Landlord/Owner cannot apply for such an order before the Notice to Terminate has run out, i.e. the Date for Possession.

(2) A Tenant/Sharer who does not know if he has any right to remain in possession after the Notice to Terminate runs out can obtain advice from a solicitor. Help with all or part of the cost of legal advice and assistance may be available under the Legal Aid Scheme. The Tenant/Sharer should also be able to obtain information from a Citizens Advice Bureau, a Housing Aid Centre or a rent officer.

OFFER TO PURCHASE PROPERTY

Date _____

To _____

_____

_____

Re _____

Dear _____

Following my inspection of the above-named property, I am prepared to offer the sum of

£ _____ for your existing lease, on the following terms:

1.   Receipt of a satisfactory survey from my surveyors.

2.   Receipt of my solicitor's advice on the terms of the lease, confirming that it contains no provisions adverse to my interests and that it is a lease for _____ years from_____ _____ at a ground rent of £ _____ per annum payable quarterly in advance (reviewable every three years, the next review being in _____ 19____).

3.   Your giving us vacant possession by _____ 19 ___.

My company's solicitors are Messrs. _____ , to whom I have sent a copy of this letter. Please instruct your solicitors to send a draft contract to my solicitors. I hope we are able to proceed to a swift exchange of contracts.

Yours sincerely

_____

Name _____

Address _____

_____

Tel. _____

OPTION ASSIGNMENT

THIS AGREEMENT is made the _____ day of _____ 19_____

BETWEEN:

(1) _____ of _____ (the "Assignor"); and

(2) _____ of _____ (the "Assignee").

WHEREAS:

(A) The Assignor has been granted the following option (the "Option"):

_____

_____

_____

(B) The Assignor wishes to sell the Option to the Assignee.

NOW IT IS HEREBY AGREED as follows:

1.   In consideration for the payment of £ _____, receipt of which the Assignor hereby acknowledges, the Assignor hereby transfers his/her entire interest in the Option and all his/her right thereunder to the Assignee.

2.   The Assignee, by accepting the transfer of this Option, agrees to exercise the Option, if at all, according to its terms.

3.   This agreement shall be binding upon and inure to the benefit of the parties, their successors and assigns.

IN WITNESS OF WHICH the parties have signed this agreement the day and year first above written.

_____   _____
Signed by or on behalf of the Assignor   Signed by or on behalf of the Assignee

_____   _____
in the presence of (witness)   in the presence of (witness)

Name   Name

Address   Address

Occupation   Occupation

ORDER TO STOP A CHEQUE

Date _____

To _____

_____

_____

Dear _____

Please stop the payment of the following cheque:

        Name of Payee: _____

        Date of Cheque: _____

        Cheque No.: _____

        Amount: _____

If this cheque has already been honoured, please advise me of the date of payment.

Thank you for your co-operation.

Yours sincerely

_____

Name of Account _____

Account No. _____

ORGAN DONATION REQUEST

of

_____

(Full name)

In the hope that I may help others, I hereby make this gift, if medically acceptable, to take effect upon my death.

The words and marks below indicate my wishes:

I give: a)___ any needed organs.

      b)___ only the following organs for purposes of transplantation, education or medical research: _____

_____

_____

      c)___my entire body, for anatomical or medical study, if needed.

Limitations or special wishes:

_____

_____

Signed by the donor and following two witnesses, in the presence of each other.

_____

Signature of Donor

Date Signed _____

Date of Birth _____

Address _____

_____

_____

_____

Witness

_____

Witness

PARKING SPACE LICENCE

Date _____

To _____

_____

_____

Dear _____

Premises: _____

This is to confirm that we are giving you a licence to park _____ motor car(s) in the car parking area adjacent to the above premises (the 'Licence') subject to the following conditions:

(a) Only _____ motor car(s) may be parked under the Licence and those motor cars shall only be parked in the spaces that we indicate. No special place is reserved for you and we can at any time change the area in which you may park. We accept no liability for any loss or damage to the car(s) or their contents.

(b) You will provide us with the registration number of the car(s) that will be using this permission.

(c) No vehicle may obstruct the access to the parking area and any vehicle that is parked so as to obstruct the parking or movement of any of our vehicles will be removed immediately. It is a fundamental condition of this Licence that you agree that we may at any time move any car that we consider is in breach of this term and that, unless it is caused negligently, we shall not be liable for any damage caused by our taking this action.

(d) You will pay us £_____ per _____ for this Licence, the payment to be made in advance. The first payment shall be made today and subsequent payments shall be made on the _____ day of each _____.

(e) This Licence may be terminated by either of us giving to the other seven clear days' notice.

Yours sincerely

_____

PAYMENT DEMAND: PROMISSORY NOTE

Date _____

To _____

_____

_____

Dear _____

I refer to a promissory note dated _____ 19 _____ , in the original principal amount of £ _____ and of which I am the holder.

You are in default under the note in that the following payment(s) have not been made:

Amount Due   Payment Date

_____   _____

_____   _____

_____   _____

Accordingly, demand is hereby made for full payment of the entire balance of £ _____ due under the note. In the event payment is not received within _____ days, this note shall be forwarded to our solicitors for collection.

Yours sincerely

_____

PERSONAL PROPERTY RENTAL AGREEMENT

THIS AGREEMENT IS MADE the _____ day of _____ 19 _____

BETWEEN:

(1) _____ of _____ (the "Owner"); and

(2) _____ of _____ (the "Renter").

NOW IT IS HEREBY AGREED as follows:

1.   The Owner hereby rents to the Renter the following personal property (the "Property"):

_____

_____

2.   The Renter shall pay to the Owner the sum of £ _____ as payment for the rental herein, payable as follows:

_____

_____

3.   The Renter shall during the rental term keep and maintain the Property in good condition and repair and shall be responsible for any loss, damage or destruction to the Property notwithstanding how caused and the Renter agrees to return the Property in its present condition, reasonable wear and tear excepted.

4.   The Renter shall not during the rental period allow others use of the Property.

5.   The rental period shall commence on _____ 19 _____, and terminate on _____ 19 _____, at which date the Property shall be promptly returned.

IN WITNESS OF WHICH the parties have signed this agreement the day and year first above written

_____   _____
Signed by or on behalf of the Owner   Signed by or on behalf of the Renter

_____   _____
in the presence of (witness)   in the presence of (witness)

Name _____   Name _____

Address _____   Address _____

_____   _____
Occupation   Occupation

PHOTOGRAPH RELEASE

The copyright owner hereby grants to: _____

non-exclusive worldwide rights to the following photograph(s) for the following purposes:

_____

_____

_____

_____

The photographer hereby asserts his/her moral rights as author of the photograph(s), and the following credit should appear against every usage of the photograph(s) in acknowledgement of those rights:

_____

_____

_____

_____

In return for the grant of this permission, the copyright owner acknowledges receipt of the sum of £ _____ from the grantee.

Permission is granted on _____ 19_____.

_____
Signature of owner of copyright

PREMARITAL AGREEMENT

THIS AGREEMENT IS MADE the _____ day of _____ 19 _____

BETWEEN:

(1) _____ of _____ (the "First Party"); and

(2) _____ of _____ (the "Second Party").

WHEREAS:

The parties contemplate legal marriage under the law, and it is their mutual desire to enter into this agreement so that they will continue to own and control their own property, and are getting married because of their love for each other but do not desire that their present respective financial interests be changed by their marriage.

NOW IT IS HEREBY AGREED as follows:

1. All property which belongs to each of the above parties shall be, and shall forever remain, their personal estate, including all interest, rents, and profits which may accrue from said property, and said property shall remain forever free of claim by the other.

2. The parties shall have at all times the full right and authority, in all respects as if the parties had not married, to use, sell, enjoy, manage, give and convey all property as may presently belong to him or her.

3. In the event of a separation or divorce, the parties shall have no right against each other by way of claims for support, alimony, maintenance, compensation or division of property existing as of this date.

4. In the event of separation or divorce, marital property acquired after marriage shall nevertheless remain subject to division, either by agreement or judicial determination.

5. This agreement shall be binding upon and inure to the benefit of the parties, their successors and assigns.

IN WITNESS OF WHICH the parties have signed this agreement the day and year first above written.

_____   _____
Signed by or on behalf of the First Party   Signed by or on behalf of the Second Party

_____   _____
in the presence of (witness)   in the presence of (witness)

Name _____   Name _____

Address _____   Address _____

_____   _____
Occupation   Occupation

PROMISSORY NOTE

Date _____

Principal Amount £ _____

I, the undersigned, hereby promise to pay on demand to the order of _____

_____ the sum of _____pounds (£ _____)

together with interest thereon from the date hereof until paid at the rate of _____% per annum.

_____
Signed

Name _____

_____
Witness

PROMISSORY NOTE WITH GUARANTEE

THIS DEED IS MADE the _____ day of _____ 19 _____

BETWEEN:

(1) _____ of _____ (the "Borrower");

(2) _____ of _____ (the "Lender"); and

(3) _____ of _____ (the "Guarantor").

NOW THIS DEED WITNESSES as follows:

1.   The Borrower hereby promises to pay to the order of the Lender the sum of _____ _____Pounds (£ _____), with interest thereon at the rate of _____ % per annum on the unpaid balance in the following manner:

2.   All payments shall be first applied to interest and the balance to principal.

3.   The Borrower shall have the right to prepay without penalty. In the event any payment due hereunder is not made when due, the entire unpaid balance shall, at the option of the Lender, become immediately due and payable.

4.   In the event of default, the Borrower agrees to pay all reasonable solicitors fees and costs of collection.

5.   In consideration for the sum of £_____, receipt of which from the Borrower the Guarantor hereby acknowledges, the Guarantor hereby guarantees to the Lender payment of this note and agrees to remain fully bound until full payment is made.

IN WITNESS OF WHICH the parties have signed this deed the day and year first above written.

_____
Signed by or on behalf of the Borrower

_____
Signed by or on behalf of the Guarantor

_____
in the presence of (witness)

_____
in the presence of (witness)

Name _____

Name _____

Address _____

Address _____

_____

_____

Occupation _____

Occupation _____

_____
Signed by or on behalf of the Lender

_____
in the presence of (witness)

Name _____

Address _____

_____

Occupation _____

PROPERTY INVENTORY

OF

_____
(NAME)

ITEM	ESTIMATED VALUE	LOCATION
_____	_____	_____
_____	_____	_____
_____	_____	_____
_____	_____	_____
_____	_____	_____
_____	_____	_____
_____	_____	_____
_____	_____	_____
_____	_____	_____
_____	_____	_____
_____	_____	_____
_____	_____	_____
_____	_____	_____
_____	_____	_____
_____	_____	_____
_____	_____	_____
_____	_____	_____
_____	_____	_____
_____	_____	_____

PURCHASE OPTION: GOODS

THIS AGREEMENT IS MADE the _____ day of _____ 19 ____

BETWEEN:

(1) _____ of _____ (the "Buyer"); and

(2) _____ of _____ (the "Seller").

NOW IT IS HEREBY AGREED as follows:

1.   In consideration for the sum of £ _____, receipt of which is hereby acknowledged by the Seller, the Seller grants to the Buyer an option to buy the following property (the "Property") on the terms set out herein.

_____

_____

_____

_____

_____

_____

_____

2.   The Buyer has the option and right to buy the Property within the option period for the full price of £ _____.

3.   This option period shall be from the date of this agreement until _____ 19 ____, at which time the option will expire unless exercised.

4.   To exercise this option, the Buyer must notify the Seller in writing within the option period. All notices shall be sent to the Seller at the following address:

_____

_____

_____

5.   Should the Buyer exercise the option, the Seller and the Buyer agree immediately to enter into a contract for the sale of the Property.

6. This agreement shall be binding upon and inure to the benefit of the parties, their successors and assigns.

IN WITNESS OF WHICH the parties have signed this agreement the day and year first above written.

_____

Signed by or on behalf of the Buyer

_____

in the presence of (witness)

Name _____

Address _____

_____

Occupation _____

_____

Signed by or on behalf of the Seller

_____

in the presence of (witness)

Name _____

Address _____

_____

Occupation _____

PURCHASE OPTION: LAND

THIS AGREEMENT IS MADE the _____ day of _____ 19 ____

BETWEEN:

(1) _____ of _____ (the "Buyer"); and

(2) _____ of _____ (the "Seller").

WHEREAS:

The Seller now owns the following land and/or property (the "Property"):

_____

_____

NOW IT IS HEREBY AGREED as follows:

1. In consideration of the sum of £ _____ , receipt of which is hereby acknowledged by the Seller, the Seller grants to the Buyer an exclusive option to buy the Property for the following price and on the following terms (the "Option"):

_____

_____

_____

_____

_____

2. The amount received by the Seller from the Buyer referred to in paragraph 1 above will be credited against the purchase price of the Property if the Option is exercised by the Buyer. If the Option is not exercised, the Seller will retain this payment.

3. The option period will be from the date of this Agreement until _____ 19 ___, at which time the Option will expire unless exercised.

4. During this period, the Buyer has the option and exclusive right to buy the Property on the terms set out herein. The Buyer must notify the Seller in writing of the decision to exercise the Option.

5. No modification of this agreement will be effective unless it is in writing and is signed by both the Buyer and Seller. This agreement binds and benefits both the Buyer and Seller and any successors. Time is of the essence of this agreement. This document, including any attachments, is the entire agreement between the Buyer and Seller.

IN WITNESS OF WHICH the parties have signed this agreement the day and year first above written.

_____

Signed by or on behalf of the Buyer

_____

in the presence of (witness)

Name _____

Address _____

_____

Occupation _____

_____

Signed by or on behalf of the Seller

_____

in the presence of (witness)

Name _____

Address _____

_____

Occupation _____

QUOTATION OR PERSONAL STATEMENT RELEASE

THIS LICENCE IS MADE the _____ day of _____ 19 _____

BETWEEN:

(1) _____ of _____ (the "Licensor"); and

(2) _____ of _____ (the "Licensee").

NOW IT IS HEREBY AGREED as follows:

1. In consideration for the sum of £ _____, receipt of which the Licensor hereby acknowledges, the Licensor hereby grants a non-exclusive worldwide licence to the Licensee (the "Licence") to use, publish or reprint in whole or in part, the following statement, picture, endorsement, quotation or other material:

_____

_____

_____

2. This Licence shall extend only to a publication known as _____ _____, including all new editions, reprints, excerpts, advertisements, publicity and promotions of the publication, and further including such publications as hold subsidiary rights thereto.

3. This agreement shall be binding upon and inure to the benefit of the parties, their successors and assigns.

IN WITNESS OF WHICH the parties have signed this licence the day and year first above written.

_____   _____
Signed by or on behalf of the Licensor   Signed by or on behalf of the Licensee

_____   _____
in the presence of (witness)   in the presence of (witness)

Name _____   Name _____

Address _____   Address _____

_____   _____
Occupation   Occupation

RELEASE OF CONFIDENTIAL INFORMATION AUTHORISATION

Date _____

To _____

_____

_____

Ref _____

Dear _____

I hereby authorise and request you to send copies of the following documents which I believe to be in your possession and which contain confidential information concerning me to:

Name _____

Address _____

_____

Tel. _____

Documents:

_____

_____

_____

_____

I shall of course reimburse you for any reasonable costs incurred by you in providing the requested information.

Yours sincerely

Name _____

Address _____

_____

Tel. _____

RELEASE OF MEDICAL INFORMATION AUTHORISATION

Date _____

To _____

_____

_____

Dear _____

I hereby authorise and request that you release and deliver to:

_____

_____

_____

all my medical records, files, charts, x-rays, laboratory reports, clinical records, and such other information concerning me that is in your possession. I would also request that you do not disclose any information concerning my past or present medical condition to any other person without my express written permission.

Yours sincerely

Name _____

Address _____

_____

Tel. _____

In the presence of

_____

Witness

REMITTANCE ADVICE

Date _____

Ref _____

To _____

_____

_____

Dear _____

I enclose my cheque no._____ in the amount of £ _____. This cheque is only to be credited to the following charges/invoices/orders:

Invoice	Amount
_____	£_____
_____	£_____
_____	£_____
_____	£_____
_____	£_____

Please note that this payment shall only be applied to the items listed and shall not be applied, in whole or in part, to any other, charge, order or invoice that may be outstanding.

Yours sincerely

_____

RENT STATEMENT

Property   _____

Name of Landlord/Owner   _____

Address of Landlord/Owner   _____

                                   _____

Name of Tenant/Sharer   _____

                                   _____

Date Due	Amount Due	Date of Payment	Amount Paid	Cumulative Arrears	Signature of Landlord/Owner

IMPORTANT NOTICE:

This Rent Statement, or a Rent Book, <u>must</u> be supplied to the Tenant/Sharer if the rent/payment is paid weekly.

Continued on next page

1. Address of premises _____

_____

_____

(1) These entries must be kept up-to-date

2. (1) Name and address of Landlord _____

_____

_____

3. (1) Name and address of agent (if any) _____

_____

_____

(2) Cross out whichever does not apply

4. (1) The rent payable   (2) including/excluding council tax) is

£ _____ per week.

5. Details of accommodation (if any) which the occupier has the

right to share with other persons _____

_____

_____

6. The other terms and conditions of the tenancy are _____

_____

_____

_____

_____

_____

_____

_____

7. If you have an Assured Tenancy or an Assured Agricultural Occupancy you have certain rights under the Housing Act 1988. These include the right not to be evicted from your home unless your Landlord gets a possession order from the courts. Unless the property is let under an Assured *Shorthold* Tenancy, the courts can only grant an order on a limited number of grounds. Further details regarding Assured Tenancies are set out in the Department of the Environment and Welsh Office booklets "Assured Tenancies" No. 19 in the series of the housing booklets. These booklets are available from the rent officers, council offices and housing aid centres, some of which also give advice.

8. You may be entitled to get help to pay your rent through the housing benefit scheme. Apply to your local council for details.

9. It is a criminal offence for your Landlord to evict you without an order from the court or to harass you or interfere with your possessions or use of facilities in order to force you to leave.

10. If you are in any doubt about your legal rights or obligations, particularly if your Landlord has asked you to leave, you should go to a Citizens Advice Bureau, housing aid centre, law centre or solicitor. Help with all or part of the cost of legal advice from a solicitor may be available under the Legal Aid Scheme.

THE HOUSING ACT 1985

Summary of Part X of the Housing Act 1985, to be inserted in a Rent Book or similar document.

1. An occupier who causes or permits his dwelling to be overcrowded is liable to prosecution for an offence under the Housing Act 1985, and, if convicted, to a fine of up to level 2 of the standard scale, and a further fine of up to one-tenth of that level in respect of every day on which the offence continues after conviction. Any part of a house which is occupied by a separate household is a "dwelling".

2. A dwelling is overcrowded if the number of persons sleeping in it is more than the "permitted number", or is such that two or more of those persons, being ten years old or over, of opposite sexes (not being persons living together as husband and wife), must sleep in the same room.

3. The "permitted number" for the dwelling to which this Rent Statement relates is _____ persons. In counting the number of persons each child under ten counts as half a person, and a child of less than a year is not counted at all.

RENTAL AGREEMENT
(for a Furnished House or Flat on an Assured Shorthold Tenancy)

The PROPERTY   _____

_____

The LANDLORD   _____

of   _____

_____

The TENANT   _____

_____

_____

_____

_____

_____

The Term   _____ months beginning on _____

The RENT   £ _____ per week/month* payable in advance on the _____ of each week/month*

The Deposit   £ _____

The Inventory   means the list of the Landlord's possessions at the Property which has been signed by the Landlord and the Tenant

DATED   _____

SIGNED   _____   _____

_____   _____

(The Landlord)   _____

_____

(The Tenant)

THIS RENTAL AGREEMENT comprises the particulars detailed above and the terms and conditions printed overleaf whereby the Property is hereby let by the Landlord and taken by the Tenant for the Term at the Rent.

IMPORTANT NOTICE TO LANDLORDS:
(1) The details of 'The LANDLORD' near the top of this Agreement must include an address for the Landlord in England or Wales as well as his/her name.
(2) Always remember to give the written Notice to Terminate to the Tenant two clear months before the end of the Term.

IMPORTANT NOTICE TO TENANTS:
(1) In general, if you currently occupy this Property under a protected or statutory tenancy and you give it up to take a new tenancy of the same or other accommodation owned by the same Landlord, that tenancy cannot be an Assured Shorthold Tenancy and this Agreement is not appropriate.
(2) If you currently occupy this Property under an Assured Tenancy which is not an Assured Shorthold Tenancy your Landlord is not permitted to grant you an Assured Shorthold Tenancy of this Property or of alternative property.

Terms and Conditions on next page

Furnished House or Flat Rental Agreement on an Assured Shorthold Tenancy
Terms and Conditions

1. This Agreement is intended to create an assured shorthold tenancy as defined in Section 19A Housing Act 1988 and the provisions for the recovery of possession by the Landlord in Section 21 thereof apply accordingly

2. The Tenant will:

2.1 pay the Rent at the times and in the manner aforesaid without any deduction abatement or set-off whatsoever

2.2 pay all charges in respect of any electric, gas, water and telephonic or televisual services used at or supplied to the Property and Council Tax or any similar tax that might be charged in addition to or replacement of it during the Term

2.3 keep the interior of the Property in a good, clean and tenantable state and condition and not damage or injure the Property

2.4 yield up the Property at the end of the Term in the same clean state and condition it was in at the beginning of the Term and if any item listed on the Inventory requires repair, replacing, cleaning or laundering pay for the same (reasonable wear and tear and damage by insured risks excepted)

2.5 not make any alteration or addition to the Property nor without the Landlord's prior written consent do any redecoration or painting of the Property

2.6 not do or omit to do anything on or at the Property which may be or become a nuisance or annoyance to the Landlord or owners or occupiers of adjoining or nearby premises or which may in any way prejudice the insurance of the Property or cause an increase in the premium payable therefor

2.7 not without the Landlord's prior consent allow or keep any pet or any kind of animal at the Property

2.8 not use or occupy the Property in any way whatsoever other than as a private residence

2.9 not assign, sublet, charge or part with or share possession or occupation of the Property

2.10 permit the Landlord or anyone authorised by the Landlord at reasonable hours in the daytime and upon reasonable prior notice (except in emergency) to enter and view the Property for any proper purpose (including the checking of compliance with the Tenant's obligations under this Agreement and during the last month of the Term the showing of the Property to prospective new tenants)

2.11 pay interest at the rate of 4% above the Base Lending Rate for the time being of the Landlord's bankers upon any Rent or other money due from the Tenant under this Agreement which is more than 3 days in arrear in respect of the period from when it became due to the date of payment

3. The Landlord will:

3.1 Subject to the Tenant paying the rent and performing his/her obligations under this Agreement allow the Tenant peaceably to hold and enjoy the Property during the term without lawful interruption from the Landlord or any person rightfully claiming under or in trust for the Landlord

3.2 insure the Property and the items listed on the Inventory

3.3 keep in repair the structure and exterior of the Property (including drains gutters and external pipes)

keep in repair and proper working order the installations at the Property for the supply of water, gas and electricity and for sanitation (including basins, sinks, baths and sanitary conveniences)

keep in repair and proper working order the installation

at the Property for space heating and heating water

But the Landlord will not be required to:

carry our works for which the Tenant is responsible by virtue of his/her duty to use the Property in a tenant-like manner

rebuild or reinstate the Property in the case of destruction or damage by fire or by tempest flood or other inevitable accident

4. If at any time

4.1 any part of the Rent is outstanding for 10 days after becoming due (whether formally demanded or not) and/or

4.2 there is any breach, non-observance or non-performance by the Tenant of any covenant or other term of this Agreement and/or

4.3 any interim receiver is appointed in respect of the Tenant's property or Bankruptcy Orders made in respect of the Tenant or the Tenant makes any arrangement with his creditors or suffers any distress or execution to be levied on his goods and/or

4.4 any of the grounds set out as Grounds 8 or Grounds 10-15 (inclusive) (which relate to breach of any obligation by a Tenant) contained in the Housing Act 1988 Schedule 2 apply

the Landlord may enter the property or any part of the property (and upon such re-entry this Agreement shall absolutely determine but without prejudice to any claim which the Landlord may have against the Tenant in respect of any antecedent breach of any covenant or any term of this Agreement)

5. The Deposit has been paid by the Tenant and is held by the Landlord to secure compliance with the Tenant's obligations under this Agreement (without prejudice to the Landlord's other rights and remedies) and if, at any time during the Term, the Landlord is obliged to draw upon it to satisfy any outstanding breaches of such obligations then the Tenant shall forthwith make such additional payment as is necessary to restore the full amount of the Deposit held by the Landlord. As soon as reasonably practicable following termination of this Agreement the Landlord shall return to the Tenant the Deposit or the balance thereof after any deductions properly made

6. The Landlord hereby notifies the Tenant under Section 48 of the Landlord & Tenant Act 1987 that any notices (including notices in proceedings) should be served upon the Landlord at the address stated with the name of the Landlord overleaf

7. In the event of damage to or destruction of the Property by any of the risks insured against by the Landlord the Tenant shall be relieved from payment of the Rent to the extent that the Tenant's use and enjoyment of the Property is thereby prevented and from performance of its obligations as to the state and condition of the Property to the extent of and so long as there prevails such damage or destruction (except to the extent that the insurance is prejudiced by any act or default of the Tenant) the amount in case of dispute to be settled by arbitration

8. Where the context so admits:

8.1 The "Landlord" includes the persons for the time being entitled to the reversion expectant upon this Tenancy

8.2 The "Tenant" includes any persons deriving title under the Tenant

8.3 The "Property" includes any part or parts of the Property and all of the Landlord's fixtures and fittings at or upon the Property

8.4 The "Term" shall mean the period stated in the particulars overleaf or any shorter or longer period in the event of an earlier termination or an extension or holding over respectively

9. All references to the singular shall include the plural and vice versa and any obligations or liabilities of more than one person shall be joint and several and an obligation on the part of a party shall include an obligation not to allow or permit the breach of that obligation

RENTAL AGREEMENT
(for an Unfurnished House or Flat on an Assured Shorthold Tenancy)

The PROPERTY _____

_____

The LANDLORD _____

of _____

_____

The TENANT _____

_____

_____

_____

_____

The TERM _____ months beginning on _____

The RENT £ _____ per week/month* payable in advance on the _____ of each week/month*

The DEPOSIT £ _____

DATED _____

SIGNED _____   _____

_____   _____

(The Landlord)   _____

(The Tenant)

THIS RENTAL AGREEMENT comprises the particulars detailed above and the terms and conditions printed overleaf whereby the Property is hereby let by the Landlord and taken by the Tenant for the Term at the Rent.

IMPORTANT NOTICE TO LANDLORDS:
(1) The details of 'The LANDLORD' near the top of this Agreement must include an address for the Landlord in England or Wales as well as his/her name.
(2) Always remember to give the written Notice to Terminate to the Tenant two clear months before the end of the Term.

IMPORTANT NOTICE TO TENANTS:
(1) In general, if you currently occupy this Property under a protected or statutory tenancy and you give it up to take a new tenancy of the same or other accommodation owned by the same Landlord that tenancy cannot be an Assured Shorthold Tenancy and this Agreement is not appropriate.
(2) If you currently occupy this Property under an Assured Tenancy which is not an Assured Shorthold Tenancy your Landlord is not permitted to grant to you an Assured Shorthold Tenancy of this Property or of alternative property.

Terms and Conditions on next page

Unfurnished House or Flat Rental Agreement on an Assured Shorthold Tenancy
Terms and Conditions

1. This Agreement is intended to create an assured shorthold tenancy as defined in Section 19A Housing Act 1988 and the provisions for the recovery of possession by the Landlord in Section 21 thereof apply accordingly

2. The Tenant will:

2.1 pay the Rent at the times and in the manner aforesaid without any deduction abatement or set-off whatsoever

2.2 pay all charges in respect of any electric, gas, water and telephonic or televisual services used at or supplied to the Property and Council Tax or any similar tax that might be charged in addition to or replacement of it during the Term

2.3 keep the interior of the Property in a good, clean and tenantable state and condition and not damage or injure the Property

2.4 yield up the Property at the end of the Term in the same clean state and condition it was in at the beginning of the Term (reasonable wear and tear and damage by insured risks excepted)

2.5 not make any alteration or addition to the Property nor without the Landlord's prior written consent do any redecoration or painting of the Property

2.6 not do or omit to do anything on or at the Property which may be or become a nuisance or annoyance to the Landlord or owners or occupiers of adjoining or nearby premises or which may in any way prejudice the insurance of the Property or cause an increase in the premium payable therefor

2.7 not without the Landlord's prior consent allow or keep any pet or any kind of animal at the Property

2.8 not use or occupy the Property in any way whatsoever other than as a private residence

2.9 not assign, sublet, charge or part with or share possession occupation of the Property

2.10 permit the Landlord or anyone authorised by the Landlord at reasonable hours in the daytime and upon reasonable prior notice (except in emergency) to enter and view the Property for any proper purpose (including the checking of compliance with the Tenant's obligations under this Agreement and during the last month of the Term the showing of the Property to prospective new tenants)

2.11 pay interest at the rate of 4% above the Base Lending Rate for the time being of the Landlord's bankers upon any Rent or other money due from the Tenant under this Agreement which is more than 3 days in arrear in respect of the period from when it became due to the date of payment

3. The Landlord will:

3.1 Subject to the Tenant paying the rent and performing his/her obligations under this Agreement allow the Tenant peaceably to hold and enjoy the Property during the term without lawful interruption from the Landlord or any person rightfully claiming under or in trust for the Landlord

3.2 insure the Property

3.3 keep in repair the structure and exterior of the Property (including drains gutters and external pipes)

keep in repair and proper working order the installations at the Property for the supply of water, gas and electricity and for sanitation (including basins, sinks, baths and sanitary conveniences)

keep in repair and proper working order the installation at the Property for space heating and heating water

But the Landlord will not be required to:

carry our works for which the Tenant is responsible by virtue of his/her duty to use the Property in a tenant-like manner

rebuild or reinstate the Property in the case of destruction or damage by fire or by tempest flood or other inevitable accident

4. If at any time

4.1 any part of the Rent is outstanding for 10 days after becoming due (whether formally demanded or not) and/or

4.2 there is any breach, non-observance or non-performance by the Tenant of any covenant or other term of this Agreement and/or

4.3 any interim receiver is appointed in respect of the Tenant's property or Bankruptcy Orders made in respect of the Tenant or the Tenant makes any arrangement with his creditors or suffers any distress or execution to be levied on his goods and/or

4.4 any of the grounds set out as Grounds 8 or Grounds 10-15 (inclusive) (which relate to breach of any obligation by a Tenant) contained in the Housing Act 1988 Schedule 2 apply

the Landlord may enter the property or any part of the property (and upon such re-entry this Agreement shall absolutely determine but without prejudice to any claim which the Landlord may have against the Tenant in respect of any antecedent breach of any covenant or any term of this Agreement)

5. The Deposit has been paid by the Tenant and is held by the Landlord to secure compliance with the Tenant's obligations under this Agreement (without prejudice to the Landlord's other rights and remedies) and if, at any time during the Term, the Landlord is obliged to draw upon it to satisfy any outstanding breaches of such obligations then the Tenant shall forthwith make such additional payment as is necessary to restore the full amount of the Deposit held by the Landlord. As soon as reasonably practicable following termination of this Agreement the Landlord shall return to the Tenant the Deposit or the balance thereof after any deductions properly made

6. The Landlord hereby notifies the Tenant under Section 48 of the Landlord & Tenant Act 1987 that any notices (including notices in proceedings) should be served upon the Landlord at the address stated with the name of the Landlord overleaf

7. In the event of damage to or destruction of the Property by any of the risks insured against by the Landlord the Tenant shall be relieved from payment of the Rent to the extent that the Tenant's use and enjoyment of the Property is thereby prevented and from performance of its obligations as to the state and condition of the Property to the extent of and so long as there prevails such damage or destruction (except to the extent that the insurance is prejudiced by any act or default of the Tenant) the amount in case of dispute to be settled by arbitration

8. Where the context so admits:

8.1 The "Landlord" includes the persons for the time being entitled to the reversion expectant upon this Tenancy

8.2 The "Tenant" includes any persons deriving title under the Tenant

8.3 The "Property" includes any part or parts of the Property and all of the Landlord's fixtures and fittings at or upon the Property

8.4 The "Term" shall mean the period stated in the particulars overleaf or any shorter or longer period in the event of an earlier termination or an extension or holding over respectively

9. All references to the singular shall include the plural and vice versa and any obligations or liabilities of more than one person shall be joint and several and an obligation on the part of a party shall include an obligation not to allow or permit the breach of that obligation

RESIGNATION LETTER

Date _____

Ref _____

To _____

_____

_____

Dear _____

This is to inform you that I hereby tender my resignation from the Company with effect from _____. Please acknowledge receipt and acceptance of this resignation by signing below and returning to me a copy of this letter.

Yours sincerely

_____

Name _____

Address _____

_____

Tel. _____

The foregoing resignation is hereby accepted and is effective from the _____ day of _____ 19 _____.

Name _____

Company _____

Note: Resignation without giving the required contractual or statutory minimum notice may have legal consequences.

RESTAURANT FOOD QUALITY COMPLAINT

Date _____

To _____

_____

_____

Ref _____

Dear _____

We came for _____ at your restaurant on _____. I was disappointed to find that upon tasting the _____ that had been ordered it was not satisfactory for the following reason:_____.

I expressed my disappointment immediately and requested that the price of the dish be deducted from the bill. But upon receiving the bill for £_____ I discovered nothing had been done to adjust for the uneaten dish. I was given no alternative but to pay the bill in full, which I did under protest, making it clear that I would seek proper compensation from your establishment at a later date.

As you must know, the Food Safety Act 1990 makes it a criminal offence to supply food which is not of the 'nature, substance or quality demanded'. As the dish you served was not of reasonable quality I hold you in breach of contract and wish to exercise my right to compensation.

I shall expect to receive a cheque for £_____ within 10 days. Otherwise, I shall have no alternative but to issue you a county court summons for recovery of the amount owed to me without further notice.

Yours sincerely

_____

Name _____

Address _____

_____

Tel. _____

RESTAURANT FOOD POISONING CLAIM

Date _____

To _____

_____

_____

Ref _____

Dear _____

On _____ my party of _____ came to have _____ at your restaurant. Shortly afterwards __ members of the group came down with food poisoning

My GP has concluded that our illnesses were directly caused by the consumption of food served at your restaurant. As I am sure you are aware, under the Food Safety Act 1990 it is a criminal offence to sell food which is damaging to health. I therefore hold you responsible and in breach of contract. Each of us is entitled to compensation for the suffering we have endured, time off work and other expenses. The figure I have arrived at as reasonable compensation for each of is £_____.

I look forward to receiving your payment or counter-offer.

Yours sincerely

_____

Name _____

Address _____

_____

Tel. _____

RESTAURANT LOST RESERVATION CLAIM

Date _____

To _____

_____

_____

Ref _____

Dear _____

On _____ I called your restaurant and made a reservation for _____ at _____[am][pm] for ___ people on_____.

Upon our prompt arrival at your restaurant I was told that no booking existed in my name. I was forced to improvise other arrangements which caused me considerable embarrassment and disappointment.

Your failure to keep the reservation I had made constitutes your breach of contract and I am entitled to compensation from you as a result. Considering the travel expenses incurred in getting to your restaurant and the inconvenience suffered I consider £_____ to be a reasonable sum.

Failure to pay me compensation within 10 days me shall result in a summons being issued against you in your local small claims court for recovery of the money.

Yours sincerely

_____

Name _____

Address _____

_____

Tel. _____

REVOCATION OF POWER OF ATTORNEY

THIS DEED OF REVOCATION is made on the _____ day of _____, 19____

by me _____ of _____

WITNESSES as follows:

1. I revoke the instrument dated _____, 199___ (the "Instrument") in which

    I appointed _____ of _____

    to be my attorney for the purpose of the Power of Attorney Act 1971 (Section 10).

2. I declare that all power and authority conferred by the Instrument is now revoked and

    withdrawn by me.

3. I verify everything done by my attorney under the Instrument.

4. This deed of resolution is a deed and has been executed by me as a deed.

IS WITNESS OF WHICH the said _____ has executed

this deed the day and year first above written.

_____
Signature

_____
Signed by Witness

Name _____

Address _____

_____

_____

Occupation _____

SALE AGREEMENT: GOODS

THIS AGREEMENT is made the _____ day of _____ 19_____

BETWEEN:

(1) _____ of _____ (the "Buyer"); and

(2) _____ of _____ (the "Seller").

NOW IT IS HEREBY AGREED as follows:

1.   In consideration for the sum of £ _____, receipt of which the Seller hereby acknowledges, the Seller hereby sells and transfers to the Buyer and his/her successors and assigns absolutely, the following goods (the "Goods"):

_____

_____

_____

_____

2.   The Seller warrants and represents that he/she has good title to the Goods, full authority to sell and transfer the Goods and that the Goods are sold free and clear of all liens, encumbrances, liabilities and adverse claims, of every nature and description.

3.   The Seller further warrants that he/she shall fully defend, protect, indemnify and hold harmless the Buyer and his/her lawful successors and assigns from any and all adverse claims, that may be made by any party for possession of the Goods.

IN WITNESS OF WHICH the parties have signed this agreement the day and year first above written.

_____   _____
Signed by or on behalf of the Buyer   Signed by or on behalf of the Seller

_____   _____
in the presence of (witness)   in the presence of (witness)

Name _____   Name _____

Address _____   Address _____

_____   _____

Occupation _____   Occupation _____

SALE AGREEMENT: PERSONAL PROPERTY

THIS AGREEMENT is made the _____ day of _____ 19_____

BETWEEN:

(1) _____ of _____ (the "Buyer"); and

(2) _____ of _____ (the "Seller").

NOW IT IS HEREBY AGREED as follows:

1. The Seller agrees to sell, and the Buyer agrees to buy the following property (the "Property"):

_____

2. The Buyer agrees to pay to the Seller and the Seller agrees to accept as total purchase price the sum of £ _____, payable as follows:

£ _____ deposit herewith paid; and

£ _____ the balance payable on delivery by cash, or cheque supported by bankers card.

3. The Seller warrants it has good and legal title to the Property, full authority to sell the Property, and that the Property shall be sold free of all liens, charges, encumbrances, liabilities and adverse claims of every nature and description whatsoever.

4. The property is sold as seen, and the Seller disclaims any warranty of working order or condition of the Property except that it shall be sold in its present condition, reasonable wear and tear excepted.

5. The parties hereto agree to transfer title on _____ 19_____, at the address of the Seller.

6. This agreement shall be binding upon and inure to the benefit of the parties, their successors and assigns.

IN WITNESS OF WHICH the parties have signed this agreement the day and year first above written.

_____   _____
Signed by the Buyer   Signed by the Seller

_____   _____
in the presence of (witness)   in the presence of (witness)

Name _____   Name _____

Address _____   Address _____

_____   _____

Occupation _____   Occupation _____

SALE AGREEMENT: VEHICLE

THIS AGREEMENT is made the _____ day of _____ 19_____

BETWEEN:

(1) _____ (the "Buyer"); and

(2) _____ (the "Seller").

NOW IT IS HEREBY AGREED as follows:

1.   In consideration for the sum of £ _____, receipt of which the Seller hereby acknowledges, the Seller hereby sells and transfers to the Buyer the following vehicle (the "Vehicle"):

Make: _____   Model: _____

Registration Number: _____   Chassis Number: _____

Year of Manufacture: _____   Mileage: _____

Colour: _____   Extras: _____

2.   The Seller warrants to the Buyer the following: (i) the Seller is the owner of the Vehicle; (ii) the Seller has the legal right to sell the Vehicle; (iii) the Vehicle is free and clear of all liens and encumbrances; and (iv) the Vehicle is not the subject of a hire purchase agreement.

3.   The Buyer has examined or has had an opportunity to examine the Vehicle. The Vehicle is sold and delivered strictly as seen and the Seller expressly disclaims all warranties, express or implied, of satisfactory quality or fitness for a particular purpose.

4.   The Seller warrants that while the Vehicle was in the Seller's possession, the odometer was not altered or disconnected and that to the best of the Seller's knowledge the odometer reading above (tick one box ONLY):

( ) reflects the actual mileage.
( ) reflects the actual mileage in excess of 99,999 miles.

IN WITNESS OF WHICH the parties have signed this agreement the day and year first above written.

_____   _____
Signed by or on behalf of the Buyer   Signed by or on behalf of the Seller

_____   _____
in the presence of (witness)   in the presence of (witness)

Name _____   Name _____

Address _____   Address _____

_____   _____

Occupation _____   Occupation _____

SECURITY AGREEMENT

THIS DEED IS MADE the _____ day of _____ 19 _____

BETWEEN:

(1) _____ of _____ (the "Debtor"); and

(2) _____ of _____ (the "Secured Party").

WHEREAS:

(A) The Debtor is indebted to the Secured Party in the Sum of £ _____ (the "Debt").

(B) The Secured Party wishes to obtain from the Debtor security for the Debt.

NOW THIS DEED WITNESSES as follows:

1.   The Debtor grants to Secured Party of and its successors and assigns a security interest in the following property (the "Security"), which shall include all after-acquired property of a like nature and description and proceeds and products thereof:

_____

_____

2.   This Security is granted to secure payment and performance on the following obligations as well as the Debt and all other debts now or hereinafter owed to the Secured Party by the Debtor:

_____

_____

3.   The Debtor hereby acknowledges to the Secured Party that the collateral shall be kept at the Debtor's above address and not moved or relocated without written consent.

4.   The Debtor warrants that the Debtor owns the Security and it is free from any other lien, encumbrance and security interest or adverse interest and the Debtor has full authority to grant this security interest.

5.   The Debtor agrees to execute such financing statements as are reasonably required by the Secured Party to perfect this security agreement.

6.   Upon default in payment or performance of any obligation for which this security interest is granted, or breach of any term of this security agreement, then in such instance the Secured Party may declare all obligations immediately due and payable and shall have all remedies of a secured party under the law, which rights shall be in addition to any other rights or remedies that may be available to it.

7.   The Debtor agrees to maintain such insurance coverage on the Security as the Secured Party may from time to time reasonably require and the Secured Party shall be named the beneficiary of any insurance policy taken out for such purpose.

8.   This security agreement shall further be in default upon the death, insolvency or bankruptcy of the Secured Party or upon any material decrease in the value of the Security or adverse change in the financial condition of the Debtor.

9.   Upon default the Debtor shall pay all reasonable solicitors' fees and costs of collection necessary to enforce this agreement.

IN WITNESS WHEREOF the parties have signed this deed the day and year first above written.

_____   _____
Signed by or on behalf of the Debtor   Signed by or on behalf of the Secured Party

_____   _____
in the presence of (witness)   in the presence of (witness)

Name   Name
_____   _____

Address   Address
_____   _____

_____   _____
Occupation   Occupation

SOLICITOR'S CHARGES:
REMUNERATION CERTIFICATE REQUEST

Date _____

To _____

_____

_____

Ref _____

Dear _____

I am in receipt of your letter dated _____ detailing the charges for the services you have provided up to _____ 19__.

I feel these charges are unreasonably high and should be grateful if you would apply for a Remuneration Certificate from the Law Society on my behalf. As I am sure you are aware I am entitled to such a Certificate stating what should be a reasonable and fair charge for the work you have done.

To avoid incurring interest on the amount of this outstanding bill I am enclosing a cheque for the full sum on the strict condition that it is subject to the Remuneration Certificate; and that I will be reimbursed should the Certificate state that your fees should have been lower.

Please confirm your acceptance of the above.

Yours sincerely

_____

Name _____

Address _____

_____

Tel. _____

SOLICITOR'S CHARGES:
DETAILED ACCOUNT REQUEST

Date _____

To _____

_____

_____

Ref _____

Dear _____

I am in receipt of your bill dated _____ for the work on _____ but am unclear about the fees I have been charged.

To clarify the matter, please send me a detailed, itemised breakdown of the account of charges for the services you have performed, as you are obliged to do under the Solicitors Act 1974, as amended. If you intend to charge me for this please let me know before proceeding.

I look forward to hearing from you shortly.

Yours sincerely

_____

Name _____

Address _____

_____

Tel. _____

SOLICITOR COMPLAINT

Date _____

To _____

_____

_____

Ref _____

Dear _____

On _____ I instructed you to undertake _____ on my behalf.

I am unhappy about the professional [service][conduct] I have received from your firm and want to make a complaint for the following reasons:_____

_____

_____

I consequently request that you take the following action:_____

_____

Please note that I will refer this matter to the Office for the Supervision of Solicitors if my complaint does not receive a satisfactory response.

Yours sincerely

_____

Name _____

Address _____

_____

Tel. _____

TELECOMS BILL DISPUTE

Date _____

To _____

_____

_____

Ref _____

Dear _____

I received your bill dated _____ for £_____ the above account.

I am questioning the accuracy of the bill as it appears improbably high and not in line with my usage during the period in question. Please review and adjust the bill or, if necessary, test the line metering and security so we can determine its accuracy and settle the matter.

I look forward to hearing from you within 7 days with the appropriate adjustment or the result of a technical investigation. Otherwise, I may refer this matter to the Office of Telecommunications.

Yours sincerely

_____

Name _____

Address _____

_____

Tel. _____

TELECOMS BILL DISPUTE:
OFTEL INVESTIGATION REQUEST

Date _____

Office of Telecommunications

Consumer Representation Section

50 Ludgate Hill

London EC4M 7JJ

Ref _____

Dear Sirs

I am writing regarding to my ongoing dispute with _____ telephone company. After using their complaints procedure exhaustively the matter has still not been resolved.

Please refer to the enclosed correspondence relating to this dispute. I feel I have been over-charged for the following reasons: _____

_____

_____.

I should be grateful if you would please look into my case for me. Please also confirm that while your investigation is under way no legal action will be taken against me for non-payment of the outstanding bill.

I look forward to receiving your response.

Yours sincerely

_____

Name _____

Address _____

_____

Tel. _____

TENANT'S BANK STANDING ORDER MANDATE

TO _____ (Tenant's bank
name & address)
_____

PLEASE PAY _____ (Landlord's bank
name & address)
_____

_____

_____ ☐☐—☐☐—☐☐ (& sort code)

TO THE _____ (Landlord's
account name &
CREDIT OF _____ account number)

THE SUM OF _____ (Amount in fig-
ures & words)
_____

COMMENCING _____ (Date of first payment)

AND THEREAFTER (Due date & fre-
quency e.g. "13th
EVERY _____ monthly")

UNTIL _____ (Date of last payment,
you may write "**until
further notice**")

QUOTING THE _____ (The address of the
Property being let)
REFERENCE _____

ACCOUNT NAME _____ (Tenant's name)
TO BE DEBITED

ACCOUNT No. _____ (Tenant's A/C No.)
TO BE DEBITED

SIGNED _____ **DATED** _____

_____

(Tenant(s))

TENANTS' ASSOCIATION SURVEYOR APPOINTMENT

Date _____

To [The Landlord][Managing Agent]

_____

_____

Dear Sir _____

Under the authority of s84(5) Housing Act 1996, this letter is to give you formal notification of the appointment by this Tenants' Association of _____, (a surveyor qualified in the meaning of s78(4)(a) Leasehold Reform, Housing and Urban Development Act 1993) for a period of _____ months, in respect of the [repair work][building works][redecoration work] undertaken at _____ during the period _____ to _____.

His address is:_____.

Please afford him reasonable facilities for inspecting and taking copies of any documents relating to the work and allow him access to inspect any common parts in the building, as you are legally obliged to do under s84 Housing Act 1996, within one week of receiving a Notice from the surveyor.

Yours faithfully

Secretary _____

Name _____

Address _____

_____

Tel. _____

TRADING STANDARDS OFFICER COMPLAINT

Date _____

To The Trading Standards Officer

      Local Authority

_____

_____

Dear Sir

I am writing to ask that you investigate _____ which I believe has been acting in breach of trading standards under the circumstances briefly described below:

- [Product safety:_____]

- [Consumer Credit:_____]

- [Counterfeiting:_____]

- [Misleading Prices:_____]

- [Weights and Measures:_____]

- [Vehicle Safety:_____]

- [Overloaded Vehicles:_____]

- [False Descriptions:_____]

- [Under Age Sales:_____]

I am enclosing any documentary evidence I have to support this accusation. Please let me know if I can be of further help in your investigation. I look forward to hearing from you in due course.

Yours faithfully

Name _____

Address _____

_____

Tel. _____

WAIVER OF LIABILITY AND ASSUMPTION OF RISK

I, the undersigned, _____ (the "Customer"), voluntarily make and grant this Waiver of Liability and Assumption of Risk in favour of _____ _____ (the "Seller") as partial consideration (in addition to monies paid to the Seller) for the opportunity to use the facilities, equipment, materials and/or other assets of the Seller; and/or to receive assistance, training, guidance and/or instruction from the personnel of the Seller; and/or to engage in the activities, events, sports, festivities and/or gatherings sponsored by the Seller. I hereby waive and release any and all claims whether in contract or for personal injury, property damage, damages, losses and/or death that may arise from my aforementioned use or receipt, as I understand and recognise that there are certain risks, dangers and perils connected with such use and/or receipt, which I hereby acknowledge to have been fully explained to me and which I fully understand, and which I nevertheless accept, assume and undertake after inquiry and investigation as to the nature and extent of such risks has shown those risks to be wholly satisfactory and acceptable to me. I further agree to use my best judgment in undertaking these activities, use and/or receipt and to strictly adhere to all safety instructions and recommendations, whether oral or written. I hereby certify that I am a competent adult assuming these risks of my own free will, being under no compulsion or duress. This Waiver of Liability and Assumption of Risk is effective from_____ 19 ____, to _____ 19 ____, inclusive, and may not be revoked or amended without the prior written consent of the Seller.

_____

Customers signature

Name _____

Address _____

_____

_____

Date _____

Age _____

WATER SUPPLY INTERRUPTION: COMPENSATION REQUEST

Date _____

To _____

_____

_____

Ref _____

Dear _____

I am writing to complain about my water supply which was cut off without notice on _____ for a period of more than 4 hours.

Please confirm that this interruption was not as a result of a burst main and that I am therefore entitled to compensation of £10.

I look forward to hearing from you.

Yours sincerely

_____

Name _____

Address _____

_____

Tel. _____

WATER SUPPLY INTERRUPTION:
OFWAT INVESTIGATION REQUEST

Date _____

To OFWAT Customer Service Committee

_____

_____

Ref _____

Dear Sirs

This letter is in reference to my complaint with _____ which has still not yet been resolved.

Please refer to the enclosed correspondence relating to this case. I understand I am entitled to £10 for each day my water supply was interrupted and that in addition the water company is responsible for the damages that occurred as a result of the shut-off.

I should be grateful if you would please look into my claim. It is my understanding that during your investigation my services will not be further interrupted.

Please keep me informed on the status of my case.

Yours faithfully

_____

Name _____

Address _____

_____

Tel. _____

GLOSSARY OF CONTENTS

A

Accident Claim—notice to an insurance company of claim following an accident.

Accident Claim Occupier's Liability—a letter informing negligent occupier (i.e. person or body in charge) of claim for compensation for accident on their premises, which may be office, shop, railway, hospital or residential.

Address Change Notice—letter to be signed notifying change of address.

Affidavit—a sworn statement of fact to be used as evidence in court.

Affidavit of Power of Attorney—a sworn statement by an attorney that the power of attorney under which he was appointed remains in effect and has not been revoked.

Affidavit of Title—a sworn statement by a seller of goods that he has the right to transfer title to those goods.

Agreement—an all-purpose contract between two parties.

Anti-Gazumping Agreement—an exclusivity agreement between the buyer and seller of property, preventing the seller from dealing with other prospective buyers for a set period.

Arbitration Settlement Offer—a letter from one party to another offering to settle a dispute by arbitration.

Assignment of Money Due—an assignment by a creditor of the benefit of a debt owned to him to a third party in return for a payment.

B

Bank Card Transaction Complaint—a letter complaining to a bank about an erroneous statement entry.

Bank: Cheque Bouncing Complaint—a letter to a bank complaining about a dishonoured cheque which should have been paid.

Bank Dispute: Ombudsman Intervention Request—a letter referring a dispute with a bank to the Banking Ombudsman.

Breach of Contract Notice—A notice sent to a party of a contract specifying the terms violated.

Breach of Tenant's Covenants—a letter from a landlord detailing breaches of a tenant's obligations and asking that they be rectified.

Builder's Work Complaint—a letter to a builder asking that he rectify defective work.

Builder/Decorator Contract—an agreement between a home owner and a builder or decorator detailing work to be done and terms.

Building Noise Complaint—a letter to a firm of builders requesting that the noise level from a building site be reduced.

C

Cancellation of an Order to Stop a Cheque—a letter instructing a bank to honour a cheque which has previously been stopped.

Child Guardianship Consent Form—a form for appointing a guardian with specific powers.

Cohabitation Agreement—an agreement by between unmarried partners agreeing on financial and other arrangements.

Company Let—a rental agreement to let residential to a company for the temporary use of its employees, officers or visitors.

Conservation Area Tree Enquiry—a letter to a conservation area local authority requesting permission to cut back a tree.

Contract Amendment—an agreement by which two parties agree to vary the terms of an existing contract.

Contract Assignment—an assignment by one party to an existing contract of its rights and obligations under the contract to an outside party.

Contractor/Subcontractor Agreement—a work contract between a building contractor and his subcontractor.

Copyright Material Licence—an agreement by which a copyright owner licenses use of his copyright work to another.

Credit Account Application—a form issued by a business to a potential customer wanting to open a credit account.

Credit Card Company Claim—you can hold credit - not charge/debit - card company (and supplier) liable for breach of contract over faulty goods/service (value over £100). Does not apply to hire purchase.

Credit Company: Reference Agency Name Request—a letter exercising right to be advised of credit reference agency consulted by a lender or negotiator.

Credit Reference Agency File Request—a letter exercising right to request a copy of your file.

Credit Reference Agency: Further Info. Request for a Business—a letter to be used by a business requesting further details on its file.

Credit Reference Agency Notice of Correction re Bankruptcy—an example notice (max. is 200 words) to be sent after initial requests to amend/correct your file prove ineffective.

Credit Reference Agency: Personal File Court Judgment Correction—to be used to correct a file entry on a court judgment that has been paid, as proved by a Certificate of Satisfaction.

Credit Reference Agency: Personal File Dissociation Correction—to correct a file entry linking you to people with whom you no longer live or are financially associated.

Credit Reference Agency: Referral to Data Protection Agency—for use if Credit Reference Agency does not accept personal file dissociation; Data Protection Agency will decide.

Credit Reference Agency Info on a Business: Intervention of Director of Fair Trading Request—for a business not satisfied with the response it receives to its request for more information from its file; the Director will consider your application.

Credit Reference Agency: Intervention of Office of Fair Trading Request—to be used if Agency rejects or does not reply to your Notice of Correction; the Director will look into matter.

Credit Reference Agency: Request for Report—a letter from a business asking for credit report on potential customer.

D

Debt Acknowledgement—a statement by a debtor admitting indebtedness to a creditor.

Debt Collection Solicitor Instruction—a letter from a creditor to a solicitor requesting that a debt be collected.

Defective Goods Notice—a letter from a buyer to a seller rejecting defective goods and requesting a credit note.

Demand to Acknowledge Delivery Dates—a letter from a buyer requesting a seller to confirm delivery arrangements.

Disputed Account Notice—an agreement by which a debtor and a creditor agree to resolve a disputed account.

E

Electric Bill Query—a letter to an electricity company disputing an unusually high bill and requesting verification.

Electric Bill Query OFFER Investigation Request—referring a dispute with an electricity company to the utility authority: the Office of Electricity Regulation (OFFER).

Employee Let—a rental agreement to let accommodation to an employee, solely as a result of the tenant's (or 'licensee's') employment by the landlord.

Employment Reference Request—a letter requesting an employment reference from a previous employer.

Environmental Health Officer Hygiene Complaint—alerting the local health officer to an establishment suspected of breaching food safety standards.

Estate Agent Appointment: Sole Agency—appointing one estate agent with the right to sell your property.

Estate Agent Appointment: Sole Selling Rights—appointing one person as estate agent with the right to sell your property.

Executor's Letter to Deceased's Bank—(or Building Soc) form of letter requesting details which are needed in obtaining a grant of probate.

Executor's Letter to Deceased's Mortgage Lender—requests details which are needed in obtaining a grant of probate.

Exercise of Option—a letter from an option holder giving notice of the exercise of the option.

Extension of Option to Purchase Property—the owner of property grants an option holder further time in which to exercise his option.

F

Family Tree—ancestral record .

Final Notice Before Legal Proceedings—a final demand from a creditor to a debtor with the treat of legal proceedings.

Football Pools Syndicate Agreement—a group playing agreement which safeguards members' winnings.

Funeral Instructions—records your funeral wishes.

G

Garage Service Bill Complaint—protesting at unreasonable charge for repairs and requesting reimbursement.

Garage Service Claim—protesting about faulty repair work and claiming for expenses.

Gas Bill Query—questioning the amount and requesting investigation.

Gas Complaint: Requesting GCC Investigation—referring an unresolved complaint about gas supply service to the Gas Consumers Council.

General Assignment—a basic agreement in which one party transfers its rights or title to a specific item or contract to another.

General Commercial Services Complaint—claiming compensation from provider of deficient commercial service (e.g. dry cleaner, hairdresser or photoprocessor) for breach of contract.

General Power of Attorney— appoints one or several people to act on your behalf with full legal authority.

General Release—an agreement by which one party releases another from any claims or demands it may have against the other.

Goods Defective: Manufacturer's Damage Liability Claim—claiming against a manufacturer, own-label marketeer or EU importer for personal injury or property damage of over £275 directly caused by defective goods. Does not apply to building construction or unprocessed food.

Goods Defective: Retailer's Damage Liability Claim—claiming against a retailer for damage to property caused by defective product.

Goods Defective: Retailer's Denial of Liability Rejection—a letter re-asserting a retailer's breach of contract and liability for selling a defective product.

Goods Defective: Free Repair Request—a letter to a supplier requesting a free repair of a defective product.

Goods Not Received: Prompt Delivery Request—a letter to a supplier demanding late goods be delivered immediately.

Goods Unsuitable: Refund Request—a letter to a supplier demanding a refund for goods that did not suit purpose as described by sales personnel or advertisement.

H

Hire Purchase Agreement: Defective Product Rejection—a letter to a supplier demanding full refund of a faulty product bought under a hire purchase agreement.

Holiday Company Complaint—letter claiming breach of contract by a holiday firm and demanding compensation.

Holiday Insurance Claim—a letter to an insurance company making a holiday loss claim.

Holiday Insurance: Cancelled Trip Claim—a letter to an insurance company demanding a refund for a trip cancelled for circumstances beyond individual's control (e.g. illness).

Holiday Letting Agreement—a rental agreement for a furnished property as a holiday let only.

House Rules—suggested list for use with short-term bed&breakfast guests and lodgers.

House/Flat Share Agreement - Non - Resident Owner—for use where the non-resident owner of a flat or house lets out rooms to people, who share the kitchen etc., each under different agreements with the owner.

House/Flat Share Agreement - Resident Owner—for use where the resident owner of a flat or house lets out rooms to people, who share the kitchen etc. with him, each under different agreements with the owner.

Household Inventory— records the contents of a property; to accompany a rental agreement.

I

Important Document Locator—a record of the location of documents that an executor will need in the event of a testator's death.

Indemnity Agreement—an agreement by which one party agrees to repay to another party that other party's costs.

Insurance Claim Notice—a general letter to an insurance company giving details of an insurance claim.

Insurance Claim Dispute: Referral to Ombudsman—a letter referring a dispute with an insurance company to the Insurance Ombudsman Bureau.

Insurance Claim for Property Damage—a letter to an insurance company reporting a property damage claim.

Insurance Offer: Rejecting as Too Low—a letter to an insurance company rejecting an unacceptably low settlement offer.

Insurance Policy Assignment—an assignment by an insurance policy holder of the benefit of the policy to a third party.

Investment Advice Complaint—a letter to an investment firm demanding compensation for inappropriate advice.

Investment Firm Conflict: Referral to PIA Ombudsman—a letter to the Personal Investment Authority requesting forms for referring complaint to them.

L

Land Purchase Option Assignment—an assignment by an option holder of the benefit of an option to purchase land to a third party in return for payment.

Land Registry: Leaseholder's Landlord Enquiry—use if you are a leaseholder and you need to establish who your immediate landlord is.

Landlord's Notice Confirming Agent's Authority—informs tenant of the appointment of an agent to act on the landlord's behalf.

Landlord's Letter re Bills—a letter from a landlord to a utility company or authority regarding a new tenant's responsibility for paying bills.

Landlord's Reference Requirements—stipulates references on tenant required by a landlord.

Last Will and Testament (Residue Direct to Children)—a form of will that leaves the residue of your estate to one or more of your children.

Last Will and Testament (Residue to Adult)—a form of will that leaves the residue of your estate to one or more adults.

Last Will and Testament (Residue to an Adult but if He/She Dies to Children)—a form of will that leaves the residue of your estate to an adult, but if that adult dies, to your children.

Leaseholder's Service Charge: Request for Documents Supporting Summary—after having received a summary (see below) you have a legal right to inspect bills, receipts etc.

Leaseholder's Service Charge: Request for Summary of Landlord's Accounts—the first step in querying a service charge; a landlord is obliged to comply by law.

Letter to Executor—a letter to notify an executor of his/her appointment as one in a Last Will & Testament.

Limited Guarantee—an agreement by which a guarantor guarantees payment of a customer's debts up to a certain limit to induce the customer to extend credit to that customer.

Living Will—a statement of request regarding the medical treatment you want in the event that you are unable to communicate the information yourself through incapacity.

Loan Agreement—an agreement between a lender and a borrower setting out the terms of a loan (to be accompanied by a **Loan Note**).

Loan Note (Long Form)—a detailed agreement by which a borrower agrees to repay money borrowed.

Loan Note (Short Form)—a general agreement by which a borrower agrees to repay money borrowed.

Loan Payment Record—a creditor's record of payments made on a loan by a debtor.

Lodger/Bed and Breakfast Licence—a residential rental agreement for letting a room to a lodger or bed & breakfast guest.

Lost Credit Card Notice—a letter from a cardholder to a credit card company confirming loss of a credit card.

Lost Luggage Compensation Request—claiming under Warsaw Convention terms.

M

Magazine Article Royalty Contract—an agreement between an author and a publisher for the submission of a work to be published.

Mail-Order Goods Rejection—a complaint to a catalogue company requesting reimbursement for unsatisfactory goods.

Mailing List Name Removal Request—to the Mailing Preference Service, requesting the removal of your name from company mailing lists.

Maternity Absence Return Notice—a letter from a mother on maternity absence who intends to return to work, giving requisite notice.

Maternity Leave and Maternity Absence Notice—a letter from an employee entitled to take maternity leave and maternity absence until the 28th week after the week of childbirth.

Maternity Leave: Early Return Request—a letter from an employee to an employer giving at least seven days' notice of her intention to return to work before the end of her statutory maternity leave.

Maternity Leave Notice—a letter from an employee to an employer giving notice of her intention to take her entitled maternity leave.

Medical Records Request—a letter to a doctor requesting medical records.

Model Release—permission granted by a model to a publisher for use of photographs of him/her.

Mutual Cancellation of Contract—an agreement by which two parties agree to cancel an existing contract between them.

Mutual Releases—an agreement by which two parties agree to discharge one another from any claims they might have in respect of a particular contract or event.

N

Nanny's Employment Contract—between a live-in nanny and her employer; integral Nanny Job Description included.

National Lottery Syndicate Agreement—an agreement for a group playing the National Lottery, without which a group's sharing out of prize money may attract inheritance tax.

Neighbours: Anti-Social Council Tenants Complaint—a complaint to the local environmental health officer about nuisance local-authority housing tenants.

Neighbours: Boundary Dispute—a letter to a neighbour clarifying who owns a disputed fence or wall.

Neighbours: Excessive Noise Complaint —a request to the local environmental health officer to take action about noisy neighbours.

Neighbours: Faulty Car Alarm Complaint—to a neighbour whose faulty car alarm consistently goes off and is a nuisance.

Neighbours: Overhanging Tree Notice—advising a neighbour of your intention to prune a tree over your garden space.

Neighbours: Problem Tree Roots Notice—advising your neighbour of damage being caused by roots of their tree and the course of action.

Neighbours: Residents' Parking Control Petition—to the local authority requesting its implementation; backed by a petition.

Neighbours: 'Right to Light' Notice—warning a neighbour about your right to a certain level of light.

New Car Complaint—a letter to a motor dealer demanding free repair or replacement of a defective new car.

Nomination of Replacement Room—to be used by a landlord with a House/Flat Share Agreement.

Notice of Assignment—a letter from one party to contract to a debtor that that party has assigned his interest in the contract to another.

Notice to Terminate - Landlords—a notice to quit given by a landlord/owner to a tenant/sharer under a rental or house/flat share agreement.

Notice to Terminate - Sharers—a notice from a sharer under a house/flat share agreement of his/her intention to quit.

O

Offer to Purchase Property—a letter to a property owner setting out the terms of an offer for the property.

Option Assignment—an assignment by an option holder of the benefit of an option to a third party in return for payment.

Order to Stop a Cheque—Requests a bank to stop a cheque.

Organ Donation Request—a document in which an organ donor specifies his/her wishes.

P

Parking Space Licence—a licence granted by a car-park owner to a car owner.

Payment Demand: Promissory Note—a demand from a creditor on a debtor to repay a loan in full on default in instalments.

Personal Property Rental Agreement—an agreement between the owner and renter of personal property, e.g. a boat.

Photograph Release—permission given by a photographer from another to use his/her work.

Premarital Agreement—between a couple intending to marry as to the ownership of property during the marriage and in the event of divorce.

Promissory Note—a promise by a borrower to repay a loan on demand.

Promissory Note with Guarantee—an agreement by which a borrower agrees to pay money borrowed and a guarantor guarantees the repayment.

Property Inventory—list of property owned.

Purchase Option: Goods—an agreement by which a seller gives a potential buyer an option to purchase goods.

Purchase Option: Land—an agreement by which a seller gives a potential buyer an option to purchase land.

Q

Quotation or Personal Statement Release—permission given by one party to another for the use and publication of spoken words and other material.

R

Release of Confidential Information Authorisation—a letter giving authority to a company or individual to release confidential information.

Release of Medical Information Authorisation—a letter giving a doctor or hospital authority to release medical information.

Remittance Advice—a letter from a buyer to a seller requesting that payment be set against certain invoices.

Rent Statement—a form of rent book recording rent payment receipts kept by a residential letting tenant or sharer.

Rental Agreement for a Furnished House or Flat (on an Assured Shorthold Tenancy)—a letting agreement for any period of time ensuring the landlord can regain possession.

Rental Agreement for an Unfurnished House or Flat (on an Assured Shorthold Tenancy)—as above but for an unfurnished property.

Resignation Letter—a general letter of resignation from employee to employer.

Restaurant Food Quality Complaint—demanding compensation from a restaurant/wine bar after poor quality food.

Restaurant Food Poisoning Claim—demanding compensation from a restaurant/wine bar after food poisoning.

Restaurant Lost Reservation Claim—demanding compensation for a reservation that was not kept.

Revocation of Power of Attorney—a document by which a donor revokes a general power of attorney previously granted by him.

S

Sale Agreement: Goods—a general agreement between a seller and a buyer of goods.

Sale Agreement: Personal Property—a simple agreement to record the sale of private property other than land.

Sale Agreement: Vehicle—an agreement to record the private sale of a motor vehicle.

Security Agreement—an agreement between a creditor and a debtor by which the

Solicitor's Charges: Detailed Account Request—request a breakdown of charges.

Solicitor Complaint—a general letter of complaint about poor service or unprofessional conduct.

T

Telecoms Bill Dispute—questions an improbably large telephone line bill.

Telecoms Bill Dispute: OFTEL Investigation Request—referring a complaint with a telephone company (BT, Mercury, mobile) to the Office of Telecommunications .

Tenant's Bank Standing Order Mandate —instruction to a tenant's bank for payment of rent by standing order.

Tenants' Association Surveyor Appointment —such an appointment can be made by a 'recognised' tenants association to establish whether a landlord's repair charges to owners of leasehold property are reasonable.

Trading Standards Officer Complaint— asks your local officer to investigate a suspected breach of trading standards.

W

Waiver of Liability and Assumption of Risk—a document by which a customer agrees not to hold a supplier liable for any loss, damage or injury suffered by the customer.

Water Supply Interruption Compensation Request—a letter to a water company requesting compensation for supply interruption (if not due to burst mains).

Water Supply Interruption: OFWAT Investigation Request—requests the intervention of a regional Office of Water Sevices customer service committee in a dispute with water company in its area. Contact OFWAT for regional addresses.

Law Pack

Software

LAWPACK™

- Customise, print and file your own legal forms, letters and agreements fast, with easy-to-use Windows® Software.
- Valid in England and Wales.
- Works on all Windows formats.
- Includes 3.5" disks and CD.
- Save solicitor's fees and time!

ALL £29⁹⁵ RRP *Except Last Will & Testament*

301 Legal Forms, Letters & Agreements
A desk-top library of DIY legal documents for legal protection in virtually every situation. For business and personal use. Includes Loans & Borrowing, Employment, Transfers & Assignments and much more!
S610 ISBN 1-898217-28-9

Home & Family Solicitor
Over 175 documents to protect your rights in and around the home: from correcting your credit file to creating an anti-gazumping agreement, you will find the ideal letter, form or agreement.
S613 ISBN 1-898217-43-2
Available June 1998

Last Will & Testament

£19⁹⁵

Includes all the information, instruction and forms you need to draw up your own legally valid Will. For use in **Scotland** as well as England & Wales.
S607 ISBN 1-898217-13-0

Company Secretary
What every busy company secretary or record-keeper needs. Includes over 150 commonly-required resolutions and minutes required for filing.
S611 ISBN 1-898217-33-5
Available June 1998

Personnel Manager
A source of over 200 forms, contracts & letters to help you manage your personnel needs more effectively and in line with the law and codes of practice.
S612 ISBN 1-898217-38-6
Available June 1998

Law Pack *Do-It-Yourself* Guides

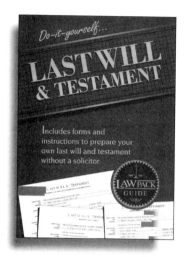

Last Will & Testament

With the help of this Guide writing a Will can be a straightforward matter. It takes the reader step-by-step through the process of drawing up a Will and provides helpful background information and advice. Will forms, completed examples and checklists are included.

Order no. B403
80 pages paperback £9.95
ISBN 1 898217 16 5

Divorce

File your own divorce and avoid expensive legal fees! This Guide explains the process from filing your petition to final decree. Even if there are complications such as young children or contested grounds this Guide will save you time and money.

Order no. B404
120 pages paperback £9.95
ISBN 1 898217 31 9

Small Claims

If you want to take action to recover a debt, resolve a contract dispute or make a personal injury claim, you can file your own small claim for under £3,000 without a solicitor. This Guide includes clear instructions and advice on how to handle your own case and enforce judgment.

Order no. B406
96 pages paperback £9.95
ISBN 1 898217 21 1

Limited Company

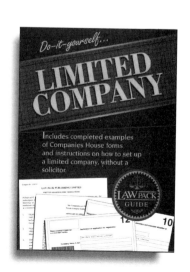

This Guide explains how to set up your own limited company without going to a solicitor. It is full of useful information and gives step-by-step guidance on the procedure. It also includes examples of Companies House forms, Memorandum and Articles of Association, resolutions and has answers to all questions.

Order no. B405
88 pages paperback £9.95
ISBN 1 898217 26 2

Employment Law

Whether you are an employer or an employee, you have rights in the workplace. This Guide is a comprehensive source of reference for anyone with questions about hiring, wages, employment contracts, termination, discrimination and other important issues. This essential guide puts at your fingertips all the important legal points employers and employees should know.

Order no. B408
134 pages paperback £9.95
ISBN 1 898217 46 7

Probate

What happens when someone dies, with or without leaving a Will, and their estate needs to be dealt with? Probate is the process whereby the deceased's executors apply for authority to handle the deceased's assets. This Guide provides the information and instructions needed to obtain a grant of probate, or grant of letters of administration, and administer an estate without the expense of a solicitor.

Order no. B409
96 pages paperback £9.95
ISBN 1 898217 31 X

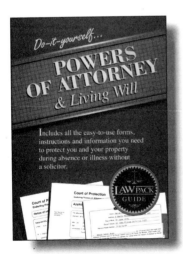

Powers of Attorney & Living Will

You never know when you might need someone to act on your behalf with full legal authority. What if you became seriously ill and needed business and personal interests looked after? This Law Pack Guide explains the difference between an Enduring Power Attorney (EPA) and a General Power of Attorney, and shows you how to create both. With the Living Will in this Guide you can also express your wishes regarding future medical treatment.

Order no. B410
76 pages paperback £9.95
ISBN 1 898217 62 9

- *Written and approved by lawyers*
- *Full instructions*
- *Valid in England and Wales*

Available in bookshops, stationers and office superstores, or call 0800 614220